G000255103

SURPRISED BY FIRE

MARTINA LEHANE SHEEHAN

Surprised by Fire

*Become Who You are
Meant to Be*

IGNITING HOPE, HEALING AND WHOLENESS

CURRACH
PRESS

First published in 2017 by
CURRACH PRESS
23 Merrion Square North
Dublin 2, CO. Dublin
www.columba.ie

Cover image and design by Alba Esteban | Currach Press
Illustrations by Alba Esteban
Printed by ScandBook, Sweden

ISBN 978-1-78218-887-2

For everyone who has ever asked
'Is this all there is?'

*Become who you are meant to
be and you will set the whole
world on fire.*

CATHERINE OF SIENA

Contents

Foreword

The possibility of living the abundant life draws closer to your heart as you turn the pages of this new book. The shy and hidden self grows courage; it begins to emerge and blossom; the damp spirit is surprised by fire and the sleepy soul wakes up to a new dawn. There are reasons for these words of commendation. Here the authentic voice, the resonant cadence and the down-to-earth experiences of the author bring a rich depth and a new texture to the meaning of the spiritual journey.

Surprised by Fire sparkles with sudden gems of bright insight. It will comfort and encourage us to risk following the call of our truest selves. The humble, honest and grounded stories, experiences and self-disclosure of the author gives all of us fresh confidence that we too can travel freely and hopefully along the journey of the soul where we so easily get lost, unnerved, fearful and hesitant.

The author shifts the focus of our search for happiness from the heavens above to our fragile, earthly condition. And, most importantly, it is in this earthly condition, in all the common encounters and ordinary experiences of our lives, that she finds divinity. Her studied understanding of the love and meaning in Christian Incarnation enables her to see this clearly – because she has long meditated on the holy depths of her own real life experiences. She is no stranger to the existential human stain that forever lodges in our best intentions; and she liberates us from the subtle prison of our false and persuasive ego.

In this, her fourth book, the author continues to take us deeper into the sacred shrine that waits, invisibly, to be discovered in all human experiences. Her vibrant creativity and her inspiring wisdom will work wonders on our faltering and wayward hearts. Telling us that now we are no longer victims, the author gives us glimpses of the enchanted place we hope one day to inhabit. And as I turn the pages I sometimes feel I'm listening to a conversation, a plea, even an argument that the author is having with herself. This pursuit of a grounded authenticity is such a radical way of evaluating our soul's journey.

It is this flow of freshness and fleshiness that gives the feel of truth to the book. We suspect that the author is personally acquainted with some of the demons she discusses; that she is familiar with their tricks and subtleties, and that she is passing on to us her hard-won wisdom, patience and trust so that we too can safely encounter those same demons that daily bother us. One of them must surely be the demon of fear – fear of rejection, of letting go, of taking risks, of being criticised, of finding and using our own voice. And as she weaves her way through this journey-metaphor on which she has crafted her book, be sure to pause now and then to catch the infectious twinkle of her storytelling. (Look out for 'Ham, Kisses and Stories' – ours is indeed a faith of the flesh.)

The author's sincere and lifelong commitment to the spiritual quest together with her professional work and research into the issues she discusses, are all impressively gathered into these few pages. It is tempting to give examples of these saving insights, but there is a seamless weaving of dimensions of the mystery throughout the book. And yet, in the end, it may be enough to recognise just one image that beckons – especially to you, and you alone – and that image will light your path all the way home.

Daniel O'Leary

Introduction

We all need to know that our life has a purpose, and that we are living out our dreams and becoming the best possible version of who we can be. We long to express our unique creative self in some wild and wonderful way, and deep down we want to know that we are leaving a unique trail behind us when we depart this planet. These desires are written into every human heart.

As the title *Surprised by Fire* suggests, this book is about the tiny flicker that is waiting to be ignited in each one of us. When fanned into a flame, this little ember can lead you to your heart's desire and to your deepest joy. Your life then becomes an adventure, where you are no longer loitering through your days, but living intentionally with purpose and authenticity.

When some of our basic needs are met, those such as safety, shelter and food, other stirrings begin to surface; questions emerge, such as 'Who am I?' 'What is meaningful about my life?' While we all get faint stirrings and hints of our true potential, we often allow them to dwindle away to the point where they become eclipsed once again. In this book, you will be guided towards excavating them from under the debris of those many layers of unconscious conditioning. You will be shown how to utilise those nuggets of wisdom and discern what they might be leading you towards.

This book will help you to begin a journey of discovery and recovery. You will rekindle the creative self that is often hidden behind the facade constructed to 'keep the show on the road'. It will help you to draw back misplaced or detoured energy so that it can be placed at the service of your deepest dreams. While each of us is uniquely complex, there are recognisable denominators in our navigation towards wholeness, and so we need heroes and heroines and great stories to help us. For this, I have drawn from some of the great mystics, writers and poets. I have also gleaned inspiration from Joseph Campbell, a mythologist, writer and lecturer best known for his work on 'The Hero's Journey'.1 He suggests we each go through stages such as 'Receiving a call', 'Departure from an old way of life', 'Finding treasure' and 'A journey of homecoming'. I have used these stages as a skeletal framework for my own explorations:

• *Part One: The Call.* Here we will explore the deep dream that echoes in every human heart, which, when discovered, can lead to freedom and joy. For example, in Chapter 1, 'The Great Yes', we will explore research findings and discover how risk-taking, optimism and resilience are intrinsic to discovering happiness. In Chapter 2, 'No Time like the Present', we will learn how living fully in the now can be compatible with envisioning a compelling future. In fact, we will discover that it is only when our feet are solidly planted in the present moment that our eyes can truly see the horizons we are created for. In Chapter 4, 'Following Your Bliss', we will explore how to set in motion a myriad ways to embrace the exciting journey of following our dreams.

• *Part Two: Departure and Letting Go.* Here we will explore how we can heal the psychological blocks that frequently hold us back. We will look particularly at the challenge of letting go of early childhood scripts; for example, the chapter entitled 'Mammy' looks at the 'mother wound' and how we may have to address this in order to move forward. In Chapter 6, 'The Belly of the Whale', we look at how integrating the dark times and facing our own shadow can lead to transformation. In our journey of healing, we will not dismiss the place of genetic inheritance, which can leave us predisposed to anxiety and other vulnerabilities, but we will discover how none of these predispositions need fully define us; in fact, our limitations may become the very fuel that makes our fire blaze all the brighter.

• *Part Three: Searching for Treasure.* Here we explore what promotes or prevents our growth. For example, in Chapter 11, 'Buried Treasure', we look at how to navigate our lives from the heart, instead of being driven blindly by unconscious forces such as self-sabotage and social comparisons. We will learn about 'the beauty of imperfection', whereby we will uncover any consent we may be giving to unhelpful or unrealistic external expectations and learn instead how to dance to a different drum, one that is no longer determined solely by culture. We will then prepare for the 'return journey', where we learn about savouring those lasting treasures such as compassion, gratitude, acceptance and surrender.

• *Part Four: Homecoming.* This is where we explore how to integrate the nuggets of wisdom and the lessons we have learned from our own 'hero's journey'; we discover that even the mistakes we have made are valuable and nothing has been wasted. We see how our lives often go full circle; the place of our wounding becomes the place of our giftedness. We discover the joy of being able to design and fan the flames of our own unique vision, one that inspires humanity with a sense of purpose and passion.

There is an abundance of literature available on how to find happiness, with some even suggesting we can find it in as little as a week or ten days by following a few simple steps. It was tempting for me to write one of those popular 'how to' books, but I felt this would not be honest for me. I believe that if we are to find real transformation and healing, we have to embrace a journey that has, as its foundation, solid psychological and spiritual insights. Anything less is only pasting over the cracks, instead of fully honouring what it is to be a wonderful, yet complex human being. I have sought, therefore, to integrate wisdom from traditional psychology, as well as new research findings from what is called 'the science of happiness'.

In *Surprised by Fire*, you will discover how this fluid, non-linear journey is for everyone. There are no age brackets here because the fiery energies inside us are no respecters of age; and while those energies change over the years, they continue to beckon us in new ways until our dying days, and possibly beyond.

Allow this book to act as a kind of midwife helping to deliver your own wisdom; allow it to be more about transformation than information. Read it slowly, putting it down occasionally to pause, so that it weaves an authentic resonance with your own heart. Daniel O'Leary has already told us about 'the possibility of living the abundant life drawing closer as you turn the pages of this book'. Yes, indeed, it will lead you to encounter your hopes and dreams and excavate your creative wisdom, but it will also introduce you to the layers of blockages that need healing (most of them unconscious). The possibility of change usually brings an initial excitement, often followed by resistance around the self we are departing from. Peaks and valleys are emblematic, so try not to skip or skimp over chapters, even if you are tempted to create shortcuts or to give up altogether. All I ask of you is that you keep going to the end; I can promise when we meet each other at the 'homecoming' in the last chapter, you will admit that you have truly met yourself on the journey – so please stay!

Readers of my two previous books, *Seeing Anew* and *Whispers in the Stillness*, have 'warned' me not to forget to include stories and real-life examples again this time. They tell me that long after theories and concepts fade from memory, the stories stay alive. The personal narratives are not sanitised and perfected, nor are they presented as 'happy ever afters', but they are carefully interwoven to help you to elicit your own wisdom. I have masked the identity of, or sought permission from those whose stories I have shared. Many are from my own experience (my many face-down moments on the journey). The purpose of sharing these stories is to help create an introduction, not to me, but to yourself!

My hope is that this book will lead you on a quest towards discovering the sacred fire that can set ablaze every aspect of your inner and outer world. So, let us go together as brave souls, knowing it will not always be easy, but it will always be in the service of your growth, and always keeping you awake enough to be continually *Surprised by Fire!*

Martina Lehane Sheehan

PART ONE

The Call

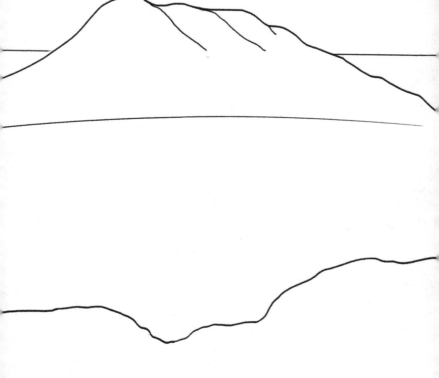

CHAPTER 1

The Great Yes

Jump and the Net will Appear

As the aircraft rose higher and higher, I looked down at the clouds below me, asking myself how all this came about. 'Let's put it out into the universe,' my friend Julia had suggested, after we had bought a Lotto scratch card. 'Yes, it is a sign ... let us go,' we said, after we had won two euro! Three weeks later, we were boarding the plane to travel to Perth in Australia. It was only a few months earlier that I had received the phone call from an Australian who, while on a visit to Ireland, had seen a play that I had written and produced. He asked if I would come out to stage it throughout Western Australia. It all felt so exciting, yet a bit scary too. *Jump and the net will appear*, I once heard somewhere; now I was jumping and hoping to God there would be a net sent from somewhere. My thoughts were interrupted by the sound of the trolley being moved through the cabin. I looked longingly at the array of perfumes (knowing they were beyond my price range). I looked at one of the most exquisite bottles. 'How much?' I asked, pretending I was quite detached about how much it might cost, but quickly changed my tone and said, 'No thank you', when she told me the price.

'Allow me,' a low, provocative voice said from across the aisle. Wide-eyed, I watched the bearded stranger as he flicked a gold credit card and then handed the perfume to me. 'So, are you on business or pleasure?' he asked, with a glimmer in his eye. Ignoring how he said the word 'pleasure', I sniffed the perfume and replied (with an accent that matched the expensive aroma), 'Actually, I'm staging my play in Western Australia this weekend.' His eyes widened. 'Oh, really, that is interesting. I am a writer myself ... I have an apartment in Singapore where I do my writing.' After a few more exchanged snippets around where we lived, what we did, how many accolades we had garnered, he handed me his business card. Pointing to the address on it, he leaned in and said softly, 'Why not come and stay with me in my apartment, and you could do some writing or whatever you want?' The glint in his eye told me I was not the first who had been invited to his apartment, nor would I be the last! I caught a glimpse of my friend Julia across the aisle as she winked mischievously. (I guessed what she was thinking: Be careful you don't jump into this net.) I declined bashfully, and pretended to nod off, allowing his business card to slide onto the floor while the perfume remained tightly clasped in both my hands. Intoxicated by the scintillating perfume, I daydreamed lazily of the three weeks stretching out before us.

The whole trip flowed like a dream; we were treated like celebrities on surreal nights out, collected by limousines to attend the opening nights of the play, interviews for television etc. We met many wonderful people and we laughed continuously. Each evening we reflected back on the day and marvelled at the abundance of it all. Providence seemed to smile on us, filling us with optimism that the next day would be just as good as the previous one. Coincidences and synchronicity showed up in the most unexpected ways; all because we said, 'Yes', and jumped into the net.

Though it happened many years ago, the trip to Australia lives on in my mind as a blueprint for possibility. In hindsight, I recognise that the miracles and abundance did not emanate from any one situation, or from any one person or circumstance (not even the bearded stranger). It manifested essentially through the dispositions we carried within us – openness, optimism and receptivity. 'The moment we choose, providence comes to meet us, the moment I take a stand, at that very moment providence moves us too. All sorts of things occur to help me that would not have otherwise occurred.'[2]

It was as if we had plugged into some greater source, which aligned us with something that felt almost magical. Though it was only a few weeks in duration, the trip provided a template for future courage. The English 'courage' comes from the French word *coeur*, meaning 'heart'. Courage, therefore, is the heart's victory over fear, and it is unleashed each time we transcend our self-imposed limitations. Some of you are probably thinking, 'Well, if it is that easy, why don't we all ... ' The truth is, it is not at all easy. In fact it is like going against gravity when we let go of our own controls and trust in something bigger than our fears. While we do not create miracles, we can place ourselves in the proper state for receiving them. While we cannot summon a supply of providence at gunpoint, we can actively cultivate the attitudes, habits and beliefs that bring them towards us. Consequently, we can reduce the power of those habits that tend to drag us back into unresourceful patterns.

In the flow

Psychology refers to heightened states of receptivity as 'optimal experiences', 'flow' or being 'in the zone'. In case you are starting to think, 'Hey, this is all starting to sound a bit "new-agey", or hokey pokey', remember that thinkers in both psychology and spirituality have long studied states of heightened receptivity and aliveness. The renowned psychologist Abraham Maslow refers to these states as 'peak experiences'.[3] According to him, these peak experiences tell us something about our best selves, where we are most attuned to a supply of abundance and providence. The Sanskrit word for happiness is *sukha*, which is created through an attitude of mind and heart, while the word *dukkha* describes states of suffering or dissatisfaction. St Ignatius of Loyola refers to states of 'consolation' (when we are experiencing peace and joy) and 'desolation' (when we are experiencing disconnection and frustration). He considered states of heightened aliveness to be connected with the divine and therefore important to reflect on when making choices. He advises: 'If the beginning, middle and end are all good *and* serve to draw us deeper into faith, hope, and love, we can be confident in our decision.'[4] He recognised a dynamism in these experiences that was qualitatively different from other times of contentment or happiness. In fact, the states of consolation, he suggested, are not always 'happy' in the normal sense of the word; they are more about being in inner harmony, fully alive (even in difficult circumstances). Through reflecting, therefore, on moments of consolation and desolation, and their felt bodily experiences, we gain awareness of where our deepest happiness lies.

We can conclude that there are varying levels of happiness:

The pleasant life – where there are lots of pleasurable things (which are inherently transient).

The good life – where you are happy with the day-to-day quality of life etc. (this brings a degree of contentment).

The meaningful life – where you are connected to a higher purpose, a sense of your life making a difference.

Of these three, it is the meaningful life, where you are firing on all cylinders, which brings the deepest happiness.

Getting off the pity pot

We all have a tendency to view people as 'lucky' or 'unlucky'. We consider the lucky ones to be those who had the right circumstances, such as a secure childhood, a foundation laid by nurturing parents and a life of security, both emotionally and circumstantially. Sitting on our pity pots, it is easy to lament how happiness or wholeness seems to be the prerogative of the chosen few.

Not having many of the foundational securities from my own early life, I had believed myself to be one of the unlucky ones. However, life gradually challenged this limiting viewpoint (especially through the Australian trip where I learned something about going outside my comfort zone). While experiences of flow or consolation are pure gift, they are not just haphazard or random; they emerge when we are actively aligned to a spirit of optimism, trust and gratitude. We can therefore actively cultivate optimistic expectations; so, rather than waiting for the next bad thing to befall us, we can excitedly welcome the possibility that when faith steps in, obstacles dissolve.

Try to remember a time you were 'in flow'. What were you doing or not doing? What were you thinking, feeling and believing? What were you engaged in? Were you alone or with others? What capabilities or new-found strengths did you harness or discover when you were operating at your best self?

Searching for Happiness

Psychology, philosophy and theology all address the search for happiness – it seems to be the mythical crock of gold at the end of the rainbow. Everyone wants to find happiness, yet it is something that often eludes us. We erroneously pin it onto societal definitions of what constitutes 'the good life', or we ascribe to it a certain set of fixed circumstances. According to numerous researchers in the field of positive psychology, our happiness is very influenced by genetically inherited traits. The random set of genes you received from your biological parents can, apparently, significantly affect your overall range of happiness. Some of us won the genetic lottery and are blessed with sunny dispositions, whereby we naturally see the good in life. Others amongst us have a tendency towards pessimism and 'glass half-empty' thinking. In positive psychology, this is described as the 'happiness set point'. According to some researchers, no matter how many lucky events happen in our lives, after a while we return to this 'set point' of happiness because of our tendency to adapt. (I believe that a set *range* would be a more helpful idea than a specific set point.)

At first it may shock you to learn that we tend to continually revert to our genetically predetermined range of happiness. Seems a bit of a bummer, doesn't it? This might cause us to feel pretty hard done by when we think of someone else with a different genetic predisposition who may have a much higher 'normal range'. Consequently, we might feel that there is nothing we can do to raise our happiness levels as we lament our genetically programmed depressed state! After all, there is nothing as bad as that internal creepy feeling that others are enjoying themselves at the party, while you are left outside, your little face pressed longingly against the window! And all because of your genes? Hardly!

Surely our own attitudes and thought patterns are at least as significant as any inherited disposition in determining how much happiness we allow ourselves to have? Those many beliefs we hold around being undeserving or unworthy can create a subtle 'bah humbug' in relation to life's pleasures. We can even get strangely comfortable with this very stingy supply of happiness and abundance. Therefore, while it is important to be aware of how we might have inherited unresourceful dispositions, we do not have to wait fatalistically for a genetic time bomb to go off; there is much we can do to increase our happiness and well-being. We can begin by understanding how much our own maladaptive strategies can affect us negatively, and how we can do a huge amount to change them. We can let go our anorexic stance and begin asking for divine nourishment and abundance ... ask and you shall receive.

The 40 per cent solution

Research in positive psychology suggests that while around 50 per cent of our happiness levels are influenced by genetic components, only 10 per cent are attributable to external circumstances, despite the huge amount of energy we invest in ensuring we drive the best car, buy the biggest house etc. The remaining 40 per cent is something we can cultivate through committing to life-giving choices and intentional activity congruent with our values. Maybe scripture is telling us the same thing when it advises us not to worry about material things (the 10 per cent) but to seek first the things of the soul (life-giving choices) (Mt 6: 33).

Numerous studies tell us that when we integrate more resourceful habits in our thoughts, attitudes and behavioural choices, we can increase our level of happiness in a sustainable way. Sonja Lyubomirsky, a renowned researcher in the field of positive psychology, refers to this as 'the 40 per cent solution'.[5] This points towards our ability to choose beliefs, attitudes, values and activities whereby we use our gifts and talents to create a meaningful life. We can also choose to heal the early memories that may have caused emotional shutdown. (This will be addressed in Part Two of this book.)

From what I have explored in psychology, and what I have learned from my own life, and from the life of my clients in counselling and spiritual direction, I would conclude that this 40 per cent necessitates that we live with a degree of uncertainty, a willingness to live with the complexity of life, an ability to trust and to take risks and to stop trying to control the uncontrollable! It requires an ability to deal with setbacks in such a way that they become opportunities for learning. It invites us to practise altruism, drawing us to live a bigger life where, alongside caring for ourselves, we actively contribute to the well-being of others and of the planet.

Psychologist Martin Seligman, who, since the year 2000, has been promoting the field of positive psychology, tells us that 'happiness is not just about obtaining momentary subjective states. Happiness also includes the idea that one's life has been authentic.'[6] He explored, in depth, those thoughts and behaviours that serve to give people a sense of purpose and which, therefore, help to maintain people's happiness. Among them are:

- counting one's blessings
- setting goals to help us develop our strength

- practising a religious faith that gives us meaning
- engaging in activities that help humanity
- avoiding obsessive rumination or comparisons with others.

I decided to ask a few 'happy people' what they thought. Most of them said that an attitude of gratitude is a prerequisite to experiencing happiness. In fact, many said it even helps to be grateful when we are experiencing difficulties or challenges.

Really? Yes, I too felt a bit dubious about that one. What about the therapeutic benefit of having a good old rant instead? However, gratitude can help access good in a difficult situation. Gratitude is rather like a vaccine, a reliable preventative for many kinds of depression.

While, therefore, we have predispositions that may make us more vulnerable towards such things as anxiety, one of the most exciting discoveries of this era is that we can change our lives (according to findings in neuroplasticity, we can even alter our brain structure). These changes can come about through an intentional and dedicated changing of our attitudes, habits etc.

When we activate our energy for life, it is like the acorn mobilising itself towards the oak, the mustard seed towards the mighty tree, the dancer towards the dance, the clay towards the hands of the potter. Our sleeping souls uncurl and turn towards the light as every part of our being and even our immune system are enlivened. While I had to journey as far as Australia to discover some of these lessons, each new dawn tells us we can rise again because it is never too late to exchange mediocrity for the miraculous. As one elderly woman said to me, 'I want to learn these things so I don't die with the fire still inside me.' Perhaps you are reading this because you don't want to exit with the poetry, or the music or the love still inside you.

A relentless force

The Olympic athlete grasps the flaming torch and carries it with all his might before passing it on. Likewise, we are called to take hold of the spark we are each given; we are called to carry it for a while, allowing it to blaze brightly before passing it on to those who are coming after us. Unlike the Olympic athletes, this fire is not 'handed' to us from external sources, but rises from within, where it animates us and moves us forward. Maybe this has something to do with what the ancient Greeks refer to as our *daemon,* or our indwelling spirit. In psychological terms, we say it is 'our true self'. Once we see it, we can never again 'un-see' it (although we can certainly neglect or ignore it).

Even if, therefore, you did not inherit the happy gene, or do not enjoy many of the world's lucky circumstances, you have a compelling life force, a divine dream within, one that refuses to be aborted. This inner orientation towards life continually seeks entry into your consciousness. Just as the snowdrop emerges through the hard ground after the winter, time and time again we heroically re-emerge from our own hard ground situations. Something in us relentlessly chooses life and light. When you fully awaken to this exquisite reality, you not only increase your resilience, you also help raise the vibrational energy of those around you: in fact you become a bridge that allows others to also cross over from stuck-ness to freedom.

The film *Billy Elliott* tells the story of a young boy, the son of a coal miner, who wants to be a professional dancer. At the interview for the ballet school, he describes a relentless fire inside of him: 'It starts stiff and that, but once I get going then I – like – forget everything and sort of disappear. Like I feel a change in my whole body. There's fire in me. I'm just there, flyin' like a bird, like electricity, yeah, like electricity.'

For us it also 'starts stiff and that' until we know that the spark that has been ignited cannot now be quenched, and we 'sort of disappear' as we ourselves become fire.

Stepping into the fire

Once we embark on the journey of finding our flame, life can no longer be seen as a mere haphazard or random string of lucky or unlucky events. Scripture tells us it is an indwelling divine spark, which is not timid but powerful, and it is our responsibility to fan it into flame (2 Tim 1: 6). We are called, therefore, to be continually open to transformation, whereby we allow the past to become the compost that produces new growth for the present and a compelling vision for the future. Seen in this way, nothing is wasted; mistakes can be turned to key lessons, obstacles and setbacks can be turned to opportunities. There is, after all, nothing like that joyous thump in the heart when we have unburdened ourselves of an old negative habit or dared to take a new risk. Every snowdrop, every blade of grass, every tiny insect is sharing this life force with you, as all creation seeks life, emergence and growth. We have, moving within us, a dynamic force, which Dante tells us also 'moves the sun and other stars'. We are part of the flame that sparked the universe into being; the same energy that lit the sun, breathed the planets into orbit and ignites new dreams in the human heart. We have to be spark throwers in a universe that longs for hope. George Bernard Shaw tells us we have to burn our light brightly because we have it for only a short while before passing it on to future generations: 'Life is no brief candle for me. It is a sort of splendid torch which I have got hold of for the moment before handing it to future generations.'[7]

CHAPTER 2

No Time Like the Present

Releasing the Mind, Opening the Heart

She was sitting looking out the window, folding and unfolding her handkerchief. She smiled continually, but it wasn't a smile that reached her piercing blue eyes. It was more like an appeasement, a sort of apology, as if she was hoping that I would somehow approve of her more than she approved of herself. 'The reason I am here for counselling,' she explained, 'is to try prepare myself for death and dying.' She began each sentence with 'The problem with me is ...', or, 'What's wrong with me is ...'. She repeatedly explained what was 'wrong' with her. She obviously believed that there was something intrinsically flawed about her, and had held on to that belief all of her life. She explained how, for most of her life, she had avoided taking any risks, staying instead within a prescribed range of possibilities dictated by her low self-worth. Now, in the late autumn of her life, she was full of regrets around her many unlived years. 'It was because I was hurt as a child,' she said, in a low, muted voice, explaining how she was still 'damaged by the memories'. It was clear that this narrative had woven itself into her very identity and had created a lot of anxiety in her mind. I mirrored back the sentences that she was using to describe herself. 'Damaged goods' was how she saw herself. With a sudden clarity, she stood upright and said defiantly, 'I was hurt in my childhood, that is a true fact, but the belief that there is something wrong with me is a thought in my head.' 'Yes,' she said, more loudly now, 'I am *not* damaged goods.' On hearing herself say these words, she allowed a space to emerge between her true self and the story in her head; she touched her own truth and her essence. She recognised that if she changed the narrative in her mind, she could begin to change her life. Now instead of preparing for death, she began to recalibrate her life. No longer asking herself what was 'wrong' with her, she began to ask a completely different set of questions, such as: Who am I? What am I here for? How can I heal my heart? What is my deepest desire?

Less than six months later, she went back to study – she chose to 're-fire' rather than retire, assigning her own meaning to maturing in years. She is still firing on all cylinders, and baffling those who say, 'Aren't you great for your age?'

Re-firing
It is never too late to excavate the dream and to receive back the years that 'the locusts have eaten' (Joel 2: 25). We get old before our time when we fail to live from

our authentic selves. Our psychic make-up is complex – our ego is cunning in convincing us that we are not good enough and so must keep inflating that ego and proving our worth, while our soul selves are running on empty. When our minds are always racing with negative self-talk, we lose our connection with the core of our being and become estranged from our hearts. We do not hear the important things when we are continually in emergency mode, with busy lives and busy minds. We mistakenly turn towards external objects and projects, while soaking up the world's applause to compensate for the emptiness inside. Afraid that we do not have enough or that *we are not enough*, we keep pushing and proving, trying to get away from our perception of being flawed or damaged. Eventually we become intoxicated from bingeing on social comparisons and keeping up with the Joneses. We feel homesick when we discover that we have travelled far away from our own true centre.

Busy minds, busy lives

Too much busyness can prevent us having enough stillness for the long-distance vision – it can drain our creative juices. In keeping the show on the road, barrelling through our days, we often find ourselves tick-boxing our lives, in what people sometimes say feels like one damn thing after another. We tire ourselves out by chasing all those illusions of success, those from which one day we will become separated. It is tempting to buy into a culture where we live habitually in the fast lane. Ronald Rolheiser puts it well: 'We end up as good people, but as people who are not very deep; not bad, just busy; not immoral, just distracted; not lacking in soul, just preoccupied; not disdaining depth, just never doing the things to get us there.'[8] The surest way to take a detour from living a flourishing life is to stay in your head, going round in circles with 'could have', 'would have', 'should have'. When you are continually distracted like this, your energy becomes dissipated and unfocused. When you awaken to the fact that the mental chatter in your head is not your essence, you begin to recognise yourself as its observer, not its victim. When it no longer occupies the whole dance floor, you have space to hear the voice of your 'soul self'. The constellation of limiting thoughts or beliefs will no longer encapsulate your reality as you begin to navigate your life towards your heart's desire.

Nature is one of the most powerful ways of discovering that we are more than this treadmill in the mind. When you are close to nature you sense, smell and intuit an indwelling force of life flowing naturally in all of creation – including you.

Nature calling

As I stared out the window that morning in early June, I vowed I would never miss another spring by obsessing with the mental movie-making in my mind. There were only a few white sprinkles left, confetti from the bouquet of spring. Each year they shyly arrived, never intruding, gifting the countryside with Heaven's petals. Somehow, I didn't notice them that year and now, sadly, they were departing. Why had I not seen them? Had I been so imprisoned by my busy life, silenced into servitude by life's constant demands, which I failed to see? I must have been asleep that spring, or maybe I was still caught in winter or rushing ahead into summer and so had missed Heaven's transfusion of beauty as I passed by each day. I had been so busy driving to and from work while planning my to-do lists, my mind worrying about a future that rarely happened as anticipated or ruminating over a past that had already gone, that I had not noticed those pearly white necklaces strewn along the ditch, longing to delight me. They beckoned for my attention and I never saw them; I had missed the cathedrals of white and pink miracles while I worshipped at the altar of efficiency, bowing before the many gods of reputation and respectability.

It is only when we begin to lose our minds and open our hearts that we begin to notice, not just the miracle of the whitethorns, but also the miracle of our lives.

In the Old Testament, the Book of Exodus describes an encounter that Moses had one day while tending his flock on the mountainside. He turned aside and suddenly witnessed a burning bush, and when he paid closer attention, he heard a voice. He was invited to stand barefoot: 'Take off your sandals, for the place where you are standing is holy ground' (Ex 3: 5). He was certainly surprised by fire! When we turn aside to the burning bushes (or the whitethorn bushes) all around us, we too must remove our shoes; we must listen carefully because the divine fire may be sparking a new dream in us.

The Kerry poet and philosopher John Moriarty was known to have spent long periods in stillness and reflection, especially when close to nature in Connemara. When I was working in County Galway, I frequently attended his poetry and reflective evenings. These few lines continue to echo in my mind and in many people's minds: 'Clear days bring the mountains to my doorstep, calm nights give the rivers their say; the wind puts its hand on my shoulders some evenings, I stop what I am doing and I go the soul's way.'[9] The gospel tells us that the prodigal son also discovered that he had to stop what he was doing and go the soul's way. He knew he had to 'leave this place' when he 'came to his senses' (Lk 15: 11–32). Likewise, when we come to our senses in the stillness, we too might hear the call to leave some place of doubt or pessimism and, instead, 'go the soul's way'. We might encounter some unexpected burning bushes, igniting some important questions: Who are you? Why are you here? What is your heart's longing? What is it that breathes fire into your very being?

No time like the present

We live in a culture where, unless you can measure something it has no value; in fact, it is considered not to exist. Perhaps it is because of this that a new upsurge of interest in mindfulness has emerged. Jon Kabat-Zinn, a pioneer of mindfulness programmes, describes how we are more than the thinking part of our mind. He says that 'when you look at thoughts as just thoughts, purposefully not reacting to their content and to their emotional charge, you become at least a little freer from their attraction or repulsion'.[10] The 'thinking mind' is only one aspect of who we are, but we tend to live habitually in that compartment. This may cause us to become restricted and stale in how we perceive the world. The residues of yesterday invade and contaminate the freshness of today, causing us to lose our capacity for delight. Mindfulness is about living each moment fully as it unfolds; therefore it is both a meditative practice and a way of life. The word 'mindfulness' means 'lucid awareness'. The practice of becoming still can shed a lucid awareness on the myriad habitual and ruminative mental activities that continually prevent us from seeing clearly. Right now is the only sane place. Yesterday may have been full of pain, you may have been awake all night worried about the addiction of a loved one, tomorrow the money may run out, but right now, you are okay; you are breathing in and out.

Heartfulness

Scientists tell us about brain hemispheres and how we can transition from logic brain to artist brain when we slow down our breathing and become still. The artist brain cannot be accessed when the mind is constantly whirring. When we still ourselves, we access more creative solutions to our lives – we begin to touch the creative power that resides within us, yet has its source beyond us.

While scientific studies have demonstrated the numerous health benefits of practising mindfulness, we need to integrate it in such a way that the practice does not become mechanical or self-involved. Thomas Merton is said to have advised that meditative practice must lead to something beyond the self; otherwise, he says, we might end up making contemplative faces at ourselves in the mirror! While we need to learn to be mindful, we can also learn to be 'heartful'; connected to the thump of life where a dormant creative spark awaits our rekindling. Some people, erroneously, consider living in the moment and planning the future to be diametrically opposed. This need not be the case; we can find a way of keeping our feet firmly planted in the here and now, while also envisioning future horizons of possibility. This requires the skill of living fully in this present moment, inhaling and savouring every bit of it, while at the same time passionately attending to what is unfolding. When infused with a dream and a sense of purpose, our daily activities can then become a series of meditative moments, anchoring us to the now while navigating us towards the new. This allows us to interweave the mundane and the miraculous, the present and the possible.

The deep dream

We all have a core dream written in our hearts. It often lies below the surface of our consciousness, below the daily concerns and preoccupations, becoming accessible only when we stop and listen. St Ignatius of Loyola had a complete turnaround through a time of enforced inactivity when he shattered his leg in battle. As a soldier he had been filled with vain ambition. Through reading scripture and the lives of the saints, his heart awakened and he discerned a new dream where he became a soldier for Christ instead. The authors of a discernment handbook, *Sleeping with Bread*, suggest that we each have 'sealed orders', a unique purpose and giftedness that we are sent to earth with. These are not so much in the domain of the mind, but are embodied, whereby a 'sense of rightness expresses itself physiologically because the purpose of our life is built into the very cells of our body'.[11] They suggest that when we become still, we ask ourselves some big questions. For example, if we were on our deathbed, what would we be most and least grateful for? (This is not for the fainthearted!)

We experience a certain inner clarity, and even benefit from an improved immune system, when we are aligned to our life purpose. Though we may try to distract ourselves from the rumblings of our inner world, the price of not listening is too high; it continues like an itch we cannot scratch or a gnawing concern about not becoming who we are meant to be. Something in us knows that we are each called to leave a blazing trail behind us, one that inspires those coming after us. Our dream can span time and eternity, because while the seeds we sow may not produce a crop in our lifetime, they may flourish in future generations. The very act of giving ourselves to something bigger than our little daily worries exhilarates the heart. It gives great joy to know that some day others may stand on the shoulders of your courage, just as you are standing on the shoulders of other great heroes who carried the fire before you.

Though our light can be eclipsed through adverse and difficult circumstances, it can be rekindled and reignited regardless of the stage – or age – we are at. Most people 'want to live their lives imbued with meaning and not just fidget until they die'.[12] What would help you fidget less, and live more, for the brief period that is your life?

All creation groans

Whether drawn to be a contemplative or an activist, there is a call to the wild in all of us – to those uninhabited places inside us that are groaning for freedom. The word 'wild' means to be growing in a natural state, true to an original potential. Our true self is wonderfully wild but our conditioning cages us in. The insistence of the ego that we appear sensible in the eyes of some 'imagined looker-on' inhibits our wildness. Maybe we need to ask, 'If we allowed ourselves to be wild ... even for a day, what would we say, do or be?'

The rediscovery of your wild inner self is a bit like the return of your inner prodigal son/daughter. The Buddhists use the term 'rediscovering our original face' to describe the journey of becoming the person we are meant to be. Writer and contemplative Thomas Merton says, 'For me to be a saint means to be myself. Therefore the problem of sanctity and salvation is in fact the problem of finding out who I am, and of discovering my true self.'[13] He goes on to differentiate the false self, describing it as 'the exterior, empirical self, the psychological individuality who forms a kind of mask for the inner and hidden self'.[14]

Life's coming attractions

The deep dream rarely emerges of its own accord; we have to call it into being. The process by which we do this is sometimes called 'creative visualisation'. Albert Einstein said, 'Imagination is the preview of life's coming attractions.' Imagining life's possibilities is not some kind of indulgent daydreaming based on mere wishing and hoping. Neither is it a directing of energies into something so future-based that you lose connection with where you are now. It is more a conscious, intentional and creative 'present moment' exercise. It mobilises you towards your next step in alignment with the truest picture of your best self. Of course we are visualising all the time, but more often than not, we are unconsciously creating pictures of what we do *not* want, based on our fears, rather than focusing on what we *do* want, based on the fire inside our dreams. The brain is constantly sending subliminal images, but we have to channel that subliminal activity into a positive and abundant image. Christian mystic Meister Eckhart (1260–1328) suggested that when the soul wishes to experience something, she throws an image of the experience out before her and enters into her own image.

Having a clear vision choreographs the actions you take, so that you are following your intentional design rather than allowing others to be the architects of your life. One might argue, 'Why not just be spontaneous and wait to see what unfolds?' However, while we do need to develop a capacity to trust the flow of life, we also need to be active in co-creating our dreams; otherwise, we might slip into what psychology calls 'learned helplessness', whereby we assign away our own power to effect change, causing us to become victims of things continually 'happening to us'.

Our quest towards wholeness may ask us, not once, but many times in our lives (regardless of our age), to refuse mechanical habituation and dead routines. It will ask us to pause and discern our hearts' longings so that we begin to live our dream again – and again. The real heroes are those who fall many times but get back up, a little stronger and a little braver; those who rise valiantly to begin again.

> *Though we live in a world that dreams of ending*
> *That always seems about to give in*
> *Something that will not acknowledge conclusion*
> *Insists that we forever begin again.*[15]
>
> – BRENDAN KENNELLY

CHAPTER 3

Awakenings

The Creative Force

I met up with Miriam nearly twenty years after we had been in college together. Excitedly, I asked her many questions, including if she had found happiness. 'I don't really think about that question,' she answered reflectively, 'but I do regularly ask myself if my life has meaning, and I feel it is imbued with meaning, so yes, I guess I am happy.' This was not always so, she went on to explain, because she had spent many years working for a company where staff were treated badly and the value system was based on profits before people. She had managed to busy herself so much that she anaesthetised herself against the pain of how she was betraying her own soul. Instead of working in a meaningful job, she began to recognise that what she was really doing was lining the pockets of her millionaire boss. While the company had 'used her', she admitted that she had used the company, in so far as she stayed there to deter herself from looking at her own trajectory. She had convinced herself she was happy, while at night she ate chocolate, watched endless television, gained weight, and slipped into a low-grade depression. This continued until her health suffered and her spirit grew exhausted. She finally acknowledged to herself that she had squandered her own gifts and was merely eating the husks left over from her boss's affluent lifestyle. Seething resentment lay below the surface as she became aware of how she had squeezed herself into a shrunken version of the self she was created to be.

Miriam's epiphany was activated through a series of dreams. One recurrent dream was of a red light flashing in her car signalling that fuel was running low. The dream forced her to ask herself, 'Why am I running on empty all of the time? What am I forcing my soul to put up with?' An answer came to her quickly and she knew then that she was dying inside, and needed to make some changes. Anger eventually translated into action. She began to remember how she had once enjoyed art and never felt tired when she was painting. She decided to take it up again and, not only did it provide relief from her everyday self (which had existed only on survival mode), it helped her paint a new internal picture for her life. Eventually she decided that living as a shell was no longer an option and so she courageously decided to join forces with her creative energy and channel it into what would give life to her soul. She began to study art therapy and eventually left her job. She now uses her art to help disadvantaged teenagers who struggle with self-esteem issues.

Miriam had followed her heart's desire, left her old workplace, discerned her values and followed through on them. There was now an emerging congruence between what she valued most deeply and what she did each day. Because of this, and not because she sought happiness per se, she was now experiencing happiness.

Wake-up calls

During our lives we can have many epiphanies, when we receive momentary glimpses of what living our dream might feel like. An epiphany may not always feel uplifting; it may come in the form of a wake-up call, when we suddenly begin to see what an unlived life might look like. When we first hear our wake-up call, we may press the snooze button; our preferred choice is usually to snuggle down and go back to sleep. However, such calls tend to persist. We might find ourselves being confronted with how our life is meandering along in an aimless or directionless fashion. We might begin to recognise how we are merely living at the periphery, or how we are stuck in the path of least resistance (choosing the easy route, which is often at variance with our deepest values). Sigmund Freud seemed occasionally to suggest that the attainment of pleasure is what we all strive for (the pleasure principle). I disagree! Sorry, Sigmund, I think you forgot about the deep desire for growth and purpose that is woven into every human heart. If we want to see an archetypal example of this yearning for evolvement we can look at the heroes and heroines of the great classics and fairy tales.

In *The Wizard of Oz*, Dorothy was living a contented life on her aunt and uncle's Kansas farm, but she had an urge to discover what might lie 'somewhere over the rainbow'. We notice how the favourite book character nearly always has to exchange some immediate pleasure for a more long-sighted goal. In contrast, there are usually other characters in the fairy stories: those who live a life of ease and pleasure and end up stunted in their growth (such as the ugly sisters in Cinderella). In all the classic fairy stories, myths and epic tales, the hero or heroine departs from an old way of life, wrestles with obstacles and emerges stronger, having gained some new-found treasure. For us, the wake-up call often comes when we are sick and tired of being sick and tired, but sometimes it comes when life appears to be cruising along comfortably (while we are unknowingly imprisoned in spirit). The Israelites of the Old Testament, though 'fruitful and prolific', were unfree and in bondage (Ex 1: 7).

Turning points

Homer, believed by the ancient Greeks to have been the first and greatest of the epic poets, is best known as the author of the poem *The Odyssey*. The poem focuses mainly on the mythological hero Odysseus (known as

Ulysses in the Roman myths) and his long journey home to Ithaca after the fall of Troy. In modern language, an odyssey can be described as a long, wandering voyage, usually marked by many changes in fortune or a series of experiences that gives a person knowledge or understanding. I decided to ask a few people about their own odyssey stories.

Irene lived and worked in a spiritual community, where she often found herself exhausted from the constant demands of some of the older sisters. She said people didn't respect her boundaries, but were 'walking all over her'. Many people encouraged her to take a break, perhaps take a sabbatical. Irene insisted that she could not, because she had so many roles to fulfil in the community. (The truth was she was terrified to do something for herself.) Eventually, she took a year off and began her 'odyssey'. During that year, she embarked on a journey of self-development, where she discovered that this theme of being taken for granted kept cropping up in her life. She explored the pattern and discovered the root of it lay in her story of having to be a responsible 'little adult' in her childhood. She gradually learned how to let go a little of her compulsive over-responsibility, began to build her own self-esteem and established some boundaries. Surprisingly, though she had other options, she wanted to return to the elderly sisters; she now felt ready wholeheartedly to accompany them (as against her previous way of resentfully trying to 'fix' them). Irene was now aware that she was the one who had to say 'stop' with regard to the pattern of boundary violations – and it stopped! Nothing in the community had changed, the sisters' needs had not reduced – in fact, their age-related vulnerability had increased. However, because Irene had made her 'odyssey journey', she was now returning to them with her own new-found inner treasures; she no longer felt bound by duty or excessive responsibility, but was motivated by a genuine love and compassion.

John said his wake-up call came while sitting in the accident and emergency department in the hospital to which he had been rushed with a suspected coronary attack. As it happened, it was not related to his heart at all, but to severe stress manifesting as tightness in the chest. He knew then that his relentless ambition and addiction to achievement had wrecked his health. Impressing the world by keeping all the balls in the air was no longer an option, and he admitted that he needed this 'fright' to stop him in his tracks. He attended to the anxiety that was keeping him in the fast lane, took an honest look at his work/life balance, and attended a stress release course.

For Linda, it was during her early morning shower that she received her epiphany! As the water cascaded over her bleary bloodshot eyes she began to see – to really see. A truthfulness about her life awakened in her, leading to the making of a phone call to an addiction counsellor – before she had even dressed (in case she would back out). This was the first step on her bumpy road to recovery.

Following the drumbeat of your heart

Our deepest calling is to grow into our own authentic self, not to conform to some fabricated or idealised image of who we think we ought to be. We all want to know that we are 'somebody' and that we make a difference. As we find the joy of being authentic, the joy of responding to our finest instincts, we also inspire those around us. Nearly every heart is haunted by the fear that life is passing us by, that the curtain might descend before we have even come on stage. By hiding in the wings and hanging out backstage, we often try to numb our creative restlessness, the part in us that knows we have been chosen, because to be born is to be chosen. Something in our souls will rail against a mere 'putting down the day' or a living from some addicted or compulsive false self. When we shrink and dilute our uniqueness, we lock ourselves away where the world cannot find us, and in doing so we rob the universe of a vital gift.

We all have an inbuilt knowledge that we are made for some higher purpose. We are hardwired to evolve; it is like an innate creative force that seems to be coded into all of creation.

Inbuilt in creation

It continues to amaze me each summer when I notice that the house martins have arrived. They travel all the way from North Africa to inhabit this little nest made of grass and mud tucked in under the roof of the corner of our home. Furthermore, they have to rebuild it each time it is knocked to the ground by the strong gusts of wind that tend to hit that northern side of the house. Sadly, last year they had to rebuild their nest after the strong winds completely dismantled it, leaving the tiny little chicks dead on the ground. Each autumn, they leave again for North Africa. I frequently ask myself what radar or compass is coded into them to make this arduous journey across continents to return to the extremely windy little north-facing corner of our house. What law is written into their little beating hearts? Could it be something similar to what is coded into ours? Could it be a divine dream? Scripture says 'within them, I will plant my law, writing it on their hearts' (Jr 31: 33). The Greeks call this mobilising energy 'eros'. Whatever we call it, this creative unfolding can rebirth us, turning our deepest setbacks into our greatest opportunities. This inner and often unrecognised elemental capacity becomes mobilised when we take even one step towards the manifestation of our dreams. Life expands or contracts in proportion to whether we take these steps or not.

Recognising resistance

Despite our orientation towards growth and the continuous call towards transformation, there is often an accompanying inner tension that causes numerous resistances to surface, which prevent us from taking any emotional risks. The prophets of old shared this resistance; Jeremiah cried out to God, insisting that he 'was only a child'. He was assured that something greater than his fears would carry him, 'for I am with you to rescue you' (Jr 1: 6–8). Like the prophets, we frequently give consent to everyday unconscious resistances, which can prevent and eclipse the light of our courage.

'You have to cut out coffee,' the homeopath said sternly. 'It is dehydrating and depleting your adrenal glands.' I then paid her a small fortune for the remedies and left the clinic full of new resolve: no more junk, detox from the coffee, walk every day, and take the expensive concoctions. On the drive home I had to pass through a town where traffic was bumper-to-bumper. Driving past a coffee shop, I rolled down the window and sniffed the aroma wafting in the air. All of a sudden the car stopped (which I insisted had nothing to do with me), and I found myself standing in line at the counter. 'Small, medium or large?' the assistant asked. 'Large,' I said, before I allowed myself any time to reconsider. Gulping back the strong, double espresso, I said, 'Sure I can start tomorrow.' Fifteen years later, tomorrow has never come! I continue to enjoy small, medium and large steaming-hot frothy excuses!

Something in us resists 'the right thing'; we often do the very thing that we don't want to do (Rm 7: 15). These resistances hold us back, and while they are sometimes much more toxic than an innocent cup of coffee, we continue to be attracted to them.

So how does this resistance manifest? Mostly in the sneakiest of ways; it will shame you for stepping out of the shadow or attempting anything that shakes the status quo. It tells you that you must stay 'small' and be a victim to your past or to some limiting cultural norm. It goes something like this: you work hard at something but stop just before completing it; you write a poem and then nitpick it out of existence or say to yourself, 'Sure no one would want to read *my* poetry.'

Sometimes it is our sense of inefficacy that holds us back. We might have the capabilities, but we lack the belief in ourselves. For those of us who survived childhood shaming around expressing our creativity, it will take very little exposure to make us retreat back into self-doubt. Something in us says, 'Hey, steady on, who do you think you are?' This is often where we make a u–turn. We might become mysteriously uninterested in, tired or apathetic about our journey and fall back into 'Oh, what does it matter?' The truth is – *you* matter! This is why you must look this shaming device right in the eye, and get back on the horse as quickly as possible.

We can build our self-efficacy through small affirmative actions. Even if you were born with a predisposition to self-doubt, you can gradually build a belief in your capabilities; you learn to cycle through cycling, and learn to swim through swimming, and as my husband often reminds me, I might learn to cook through cooking! Ouch! Each step provides the impetus and energy to take another step, and then another. Sometimes just one step can break a downward spiral and set in motion a series of steps leading to an upward spiral. This is how the whole orientation of our lives can begin to change.

Inner freedom

The first and perhaps most important step is to become clear on what you deeply desire – not a vague 'I want to be happy', but the kind of deep commitment that is congruent with your inner dream. Your deepest dream is fundamentally a divine dream for your happiness. This is deeper than a mere wish or a fantasy; it is aligned with your values. Some people would say it is like following your 'moral conscience', which is like an inner feeling or voice acting as a guide to the rightness or wrongness of a particular path. This inner knowledge can be known at gut level, and we generally find that going against it diminishes us (and those around us) in some way. Unfortunately, many people confuse their conscience with their inner critic. The inner critic lives in the domain of the ego and is usually an interjection from an authority figure from early life. Unlike the voice of conscience, the critic does not serve your growth, and tends to get quite savage when it senses that you are starting to grow or make changes.

When we choose to take a step towards change in our lives, not everyone around us will be in accord with us initially. We may have to choose between betraying our own souls and disappointing others, or even having to allow others to be angry with us, especially if they have other hopes or agendas for us. We may have to part company with a group or a long-held family loyalty or belief system. Just as the alcoholic can no longer hang around the pub with the old drinking mates, neither can we stay entangled with people who cannot accept our freedom or growth. In our daring to become authentic, we sometimes have to dig deep and depart from the 'good advice' of others whenever it is at variance with our own conscience or the inner voice of wisdom. There are always two cross-currents operating in us: the desire to become free and to share our light, and the fear of the stepping out that this light necessitates.

In ancient Ireland, sometime between AD 512 and 530, St Brendan the Navigator set out in search of the Isle of the Blessed, encountering many adventures along the way. Little was known at that time about anything existing beyond the great horizon, but despite this uncertainty, some inner prompt was urging St Brendan to go and fulfil his mission.

We all have our undiscovered and unexplored continents within. While you have to live out the roles and duties of every day, you too have an inner dream to set sail. Your call may come from within, or without; sometimes it is when you discover that the rug has been pulled from under you and, directionless and lost, you feel as if your old life is dying. However, a new awakening can follow this discovery; you may discover the self you have long being anaesthetising, you might discover gifts, talents or your particular mission in life. It can come as a whisper, an intuition or an inner knowing. This is not some kind of 'happy ever after' scenario; we continue to live with our human condition, but can do so with more meaning, congruence and direction.

A spirit, wild and wonderful

While we often refer to the coming of the Spirit as if it is from above, or beyond, it is often experienced as an inner expansion, a broadening of consciousness. It is wild and free and each of us hears the Spirit in our own 'language', through our own unique journey and personality (Acts 2: 7–8). The symbol of a flame often depicts the energy of the Spirit, which blows where she wills, sweeping the cobwebs from our little hiding places, calling us out from behind those faces that are not our true essence. She reshapes us from all those ways in which we have twisted and contorted ourselves beyond recognition. She removes the dust left on our souls from old attachments and false identities and uncovers the very imprint of God in the temple of our being. She fans into flame something that can leave us dismantled, disturbed and uncertain, but alive, oh so alive! She surprises us with fire and, as Rainer Maria Rilke's poetry reminds us, takes us to the limits of our longings and flares up like flame.

> *God speaks to each of us as he makes us,*
> *Then walks with us silently out of the night.*
> *We dimly hear these words;*
> *You sent me out beyond your recall*
> *Go to the limits of your longing.*
> *Embody me.*
> *Flare up like flame.*
> *In addition, make big shadows I can move in.*
> *Let everything happen to you; beauty and terror.*
> *Just keep going. No feeling is final.*
> *Do not let yourself lose me.*
> *Nearby is the country they call life.*
> *You will know it by its seriousness.*
> *Give me your hand.*[16]

Chapter 4

Following Your Bliss

The Hero's Journey

'Put it in writing,' she said, as she looked at me with concern. I looked out the window; a watery sun cast its early spring light and then shyly retreated behind a looming cloud. I walked out of her office in a grey in-between place, knees a bit shaky, as if standing at the edge of an abyss. I went for a coffee but could not taste it. My mind whirred in circles ... Sure, it was a good job, maybe I should withdraw my resignation, I liked my colleagues, and the pay was good. The memory of my mother's advice chorused in my head, 'a good government job, hard to come by these days, you need it for the rainy day'. Then came the memory of Sister Paul from my schooldays, peering over her rounded glasses with piercing grey eyes. Sure she had us all sorted: some of us for teaching, some for nursing, the others for the civil service and the rest in secretarial courses. She broached religious life just once, checking if we had 'any nuns in the family', and those who admitted that they had were encouraged to 'talk to her some time'. We were given the dates by which we should be sending completed applications for the various positions. I didn't know then where I fitted in, and I still didn't know now, as I walked out the door having handed in my notice to resign from my 'good, pensionable government job'. I did not know where, or what, the next step might be. I was about to make a u-turn, about to go back in to say I had changed my mind, but something ignited from within: a, nameless, formless intuition; it was asking that I welcome it. What would I do, pray to Sister Paul or just risk it? I decided then that *I would put it in writing.*

At the threshold of change, there can be a host of convincing arguments as to why you should stay safe – better the devil you know. The 'what if' voices tend to drone on and on: What if I fail? What if things don't work out? What if ... ? What if ... ? Of course, there lies ahead every possibility that the dream could crash, that this barely flickering flame could be snuffed out at the first hurdle, no certainty that life's longing for itself could be enough. Even after I had put it in writing, part of me longed to return to those days that were safely divided into break time, lunchtime and evening; days where often my decisions revolved around whether I would have a brown or a fruit scone at break time, whether I would stay in the canteen or go out for lunch. Many years later, I still occasionally feel a bit homesick for the life I was able to control, where I could generally count on knowing what was happening next, where the calendar was marked out and circled with the standard bank holidays, summer holidays, paydays etc.

We can get so caught up in controlling the details we often miss the broader horizon; we can unconsciously fill our lives with so many urgent concerns that we make ourselves unavailable, and therefore unwilling, to hear the voice of the soul when she calls. However, if we remain unfaithful to our true self, all sorts of neuroses can move centre-field.

The big questions

In school, Sister Paul repeatedly asked us, 'Now girls, what are you going to do when you leave school?' (A girl once cheekily answered, 'Sister, I was actually going to go straight home!') Perhaps Sister Paul's question needed to be superseded by the more elemental questions: What makes your heart sing? What is your true nature? What is your deepest dream? What do you want to do with your one amazing opportunity to make a difference? These questions are important because any attempt to override one's nature will always backfire, even if it conforms to the most virtuous or socially acceptable way of life. Deep inside, we know that the meaning of our life is somehow related to discovering how to live our potential, and how to add something beautiful to humanity. We each want to leave a daring and blazing trail behind us when we leave this planet. Anything less than this leaves a kind of gnawing pain in the soul.

> *Vocation does not come from wilfulness.*
> *It comes from listening. I must listen to my life*
> *And try to understand what it is truly about –*
> *quite apart from what I would like it to be about –*
> *or my life will never represent anything real*
> *In the world, no matter how earnest my intentions.*[17]

The hero's journey

Mythologist Joseph Campbell wrote about the ways in which the study of the various mythologies of the world can be directly relevant to the lives of contemporary men and women. In 1949, his first major work, *The Hero with a Thousand Faces*,[18] introduced the now-famous concept of the 'hero's journey'. Campbell describes the search for meaning and wisdom in which we are all invited to engage at some point in our lives. Myths are potentially useful guides in the search for metaphysical meaning. They give us some hints around interpreting our place in the universe. Myths, like fairy tales, give us a synthesis of values, which give us life and meaning. The word 'hero' provides an archetypal image; it describes one who takes a journey to find some treasure, which is subsequently brought back to be used as a gift for the common good. These archetypes come from a deeper source, what Carl Jung calls 'the collective unconscious', and are recurring universal patterns in humanity. In the context of developmental psychology, we can use the hero's journey as a framework whereby we relate our own existence to the larger cultural and universal meaning. This allows our personal story to be explored creatively and therapeutically. As discussed earlier, there comes a time in all of our lives when this call may come; perhaps when one door closes and we discover there is another one opening. This can happen through job loss, relationship breakdown, illness etc. Campbell outlines certain stages that we go through in our journey towards greater meaning. These include: 'The Call', 'Refusal of the Call', 'Departure', 'Initiation', 'Meeting the Mentor', 'Entering the Belly of the Whale', 'Crossing Thresholds' and 'The Return Journey'.

The call

We can feel both excited and resistant to following that first tug, and it can sometimes even be tempting to refuse the journey, especially when over-subscribing to cautionary voices. When we do eventually respond to the call and embrace the journey, it is often through a time of grace, often referred to as a 'kairos' time, which the Greeks refer to as an opportune moment, the right time. This kairos time is more than just a lucky break; in fact, we rarely grow through luck, but through opening our consciousness to the bigger questions and creating a readiness to respond: 'The familiar life horizon has been outgrown, the old concepts, ideals, and emotional patterns no longer fit, the time for passing of a threshold is at hand.'[19]

Experiences of grace often present themselves as a fresh insight, a 'just knowing'. It could be as simple as clearing out a cupboard, when you suddenly see your pattern of hoarding. This might prompt you to declutter your life (or your mind) of some useless baggage, which can bring a new lightness and a decision to trust in providence rather than storing stuff for 'a rainy day'.

Can you locate moments when you just knew the right thing to do or the next best step to take ?

In the opening chapter of Charles Dickens' *A Christmas Carol*, Scrooge, a miserly hoarder, crosses over the threshold of his house where his journey of transformation takes place. He gets the call – he hears rattling chains, and the ghost of Marley comes from the other world to show Scrooge his present life. Marley confronts him with how he once gave up his own dream and then forces Scrooge to look at the shrunken, miserly way he has since lived his life. The imminence of his death leads to Scrooge undergoing a *metanoia* – a spiritual awakening. Through embracing a journey of awareness, his heart becomes light and childlike, and he wakes on Christmas morning filled with a new generosity. He returns to his community and lives a life of hospitality and loving service.

Scrooge could have refused the call and taken his obsession with money and privacy to the grave. Campbell describes how refusal manifests itself: 'Refusal of the summons converts the adventure into its negative. Walled in boredom, hard work, or "culture", the subject loses the power of significant affirmative action and becomes a victim to be saved. His flowering world becomes a wasteland of dry stones and his life feels meaningless.'[20] Campbell suggests that refusing a call to growth/fullness of life causes a loss of aliveness, a 'wasteland of dry stones'. Perhaps one way we can refuse the call is by keeping our desires and dreams vague, keeping them at arm's length; we might say 'I want to live a meaningful life', but refuse to become clearer about what 'living meaningfully' would actually mean. However, Campbell assures us that the call will come back again in another time or place.

Refusing the call – my way, or no way

They were sitting in a circle, singing completely out of tune. Dementia had assaulted their minds, yet they knew all the words: 'I travelled each and every highway, but more, much more than that, I did it my way.' Pat and I were visiting the nursing home that Sunday when the pianist asked Pat to sing. The song had finished, but one old lady continued to bellow out, 'I did it my way, much more than this I did it ... '. She had short silver hair cut in a bob and a tiny little box hat placed right on top of her head. She kept a long distance away from the rest of the residents and sort of looked down her nose at them if they spoke to her. Though she was sitting in a wheelchair, she managed to swivel her hips and snap her fingers to the beat of the music. Suddenly, she folded her arms, adjusted her hat, held her head high and clutched her handbag for dear life. Every so often she took out a roll of notes and started to count them. She turned to me, extending her hand, and in the poshest of accents said, 'I own this place you know. Yes, I own this place and I don't allow any hobos in here.' (I wasn't sure if I was one of the hobos.) 'Frank Sinatra is a great singer,' she said, pointing to Pat, 'and he is very wealthy.' Before I could ask her any more about that, she continued, 'Apparently he made a lot of money on that song; they say he is worth over a thousand pounds!' She continued, even louder this time, 'but more, much more than this, I did it my way ...' . Suddenly a nurse came to wheel her back to her room, only to be yelled and screamed at. 'Don't touch me, I own this place, get away from me, you hobo; you are trying to take my money.' I could still hear her, kicking and screaming 'I Did It My Way' while being wheeled down the corridor.

We can hang on for a lifetime, gripping on to our purses and personas, carrying them to the grave while continuing to insist on 'doing it our way'. We may ignore the many conversion moments that call us to do it another way, perhaps God's way.

Times of initiation, crossing thresholds
We are often called to go on new journeys but we pull back at the threshold of change. We do this out of fear, staying instead behind the grim walls of a prison built of 'what if' or 'just in case' scenarios. We say, 'I'd better not do that now – just in case others get offended, or just in case I fail ... just in case I make a fool of myself, get criticised or just in case I can't afford it.' A life lived out of a philosophy of 'just in case' becomes very impotent, because for as long as we keep our true potentiality out of sight and out of mind, it will continue to rumble underground. We might try to hide from these rumbling sounds like the frightened disciples in the locked room (Jn 20: 19). However, the persistent yet gentle knock will continue at the door of our hearts, calling us forth to risk living the one and only life we *can* live. When we open the threshold door, it closes behind us, and then we discover a series of other doors beginning to open. It is then that we recognise that we can no more go back than the butterfly can return to being a caterpillar.

Mentors and role models
When we commit to any new journey, we may feel an initial aloneness, especially as we leave behind something

familiar; but as we travel onwards, we are often sent a mentor or a role model to inspire us, to draw forth from us an image of who we want to be. The Little Prince meets a wise fox. When Dorothy headed off to find the wizard, 'the wonderful wizard of Oz', she met a tin man, a scarecrow and a lion who kept her company. We cannot travel alone all of the time. Sometimes, a whole host of unseen helpers and unforeseen circumstances will be sent to assist us. Perhaps, though invisible to the eye, they continually applaud us backstage, urging us onwards every time we choose a new journey. Perhaps we can see these mentors only at times of crisis or transition, but we should be aware that they are there with us at every turn in the road. There is wisdom in the phrase 'when the student is ready the master appears'.

On the journey, we sometimes meet a few villains (frequently disguised as angels), who offer us artificial shortcuts, promises of stones turning to bread. In Dante's *Inferno*, as the hero begins his journey, he meets three beasts – a wolf, a leopard and a lion – each representing vices that thwart him on his journey (greed, pride and addiction to pleasure). Interestingly, when Jesus entered the desert he encountered three temptations (Mt 4: 1-11).

The hero refuses to be sidelined, but continues to journey towards the pursuit of a higher purpose and his deepest desire. Buddhist philosophy advises that our desires are often at the root of our suffering. However, we have to understand that there is a pivotal distinction between our surface/ego cravings, and the deep desire in our hearts. Scripture advises we shake off the ego and its illusory promises: 'Put aside your old self, which belongs to your old way of life and is corrupted by following illusory desires' (Ep 4: 22). Searching for the treasure, therefore, is a quest for all that is authentic and liberating; it is, as Rilke says, a desire to set free all that waits within.

> *I believe in all that has never yet been spoken.*
> *I want to free what waits within me*
> *so that what no one has dared to wish for*
>
> *may for once spring clear*
> *without my contriving*
> *If this is arrogant, God forgive me,*
> *but, this is what I need to say*
> *may what I do flow from me like a river,*
> *no forcing and no holding back,*
> *The way it is with children.*
>
> *Then in these swelling and ebbing currents,*
> *these deepening tides moving out, returning,*
> *I will sing you as no one ever has,*
>
> *streaming through widening channels*
> *into the open sea.*[21]

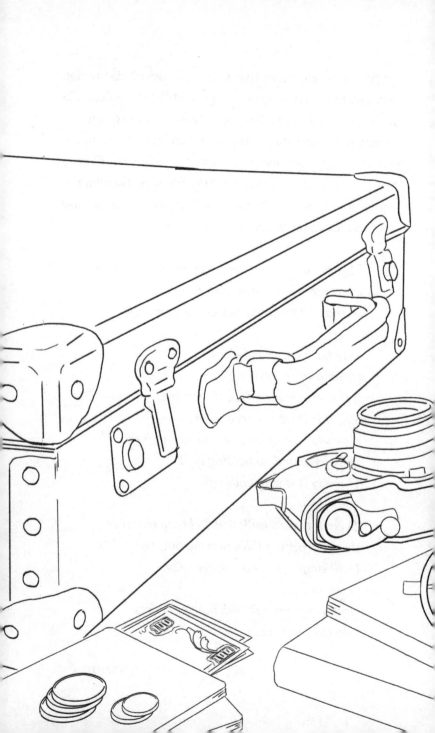

PART TWO

Departure and Letting Go

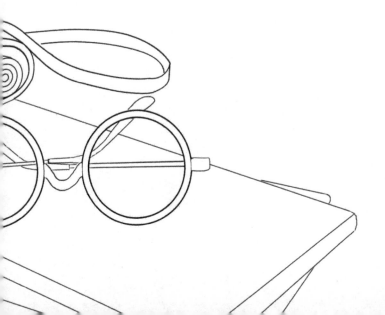

CHAPTER 5

Something Inside So Strong

Challenges as Opportunities

She came into each session and stayed for about five minutes, slamming the door each time she left. For the duration of the time she sat there she kept her arms folded and her eyes rolling upwards, as she shuffled her feet on the ground and emitted long, laborious sighs. It was the third day of the four-day conference I was presenting and I worried why this participant kept leaving the room. I began to feel a sudden but familiar twist in my stomach; a crippling inadequacy clouded my concentration as I began more and more to doubt the conviction of my delivery. I smiled at her but that didn't work either. Each time I saw her 'disapproving eyes' I felt myself getting smaller until I wanted to run home. The knot in my stomach transported me back to a time and place I thought I had long forgotten ...

Sitting between the warm fat bellies of the milk churns on the way to the creamery, I would cling tightly to the handles in an effort to soothe the cold feeling of dread in my stomach. The nearer we got to the creamery, the more my stomach would tighten, as the school was just a short walk from there and *she* would be there staring at me with those disapproving eyes. The slowing down of the plodding of the horse's hooves on the road told me the time was near at hand. I was so jealous of that horse: he could go back home while I had to go to school! As I walked towards the school gate, I would start practising how to smile at her so that she might not hate me so much today. I would pin my 'Bay City Rollers' badge firmly onto my uniform. (I didn't even know who the Bay City Rollers were, but I knew the girl who 'hated me with her eyes' was into them.) This was my desperate attempt to be included in her 'in' group. I even had my schoolbooks covered with pictures of the lead singer in the band, as I had heard her say he was her favourite. Unfortunately, neither the badge, the pictures nor the smile took away the pain of the knot in my stomach. While I did manage to be included in her group, my soul-self stayed twisted in a knot!

That same knot was twisting again now (nearly forty years later), doing the same thing: trying to change 'disapproving eyes' into ones that would approve of me. I was about to go over and find out why this woman 'hated me'. Instead, I stayed with the discomfort. Strangely, after a while I began to feel at ease, even grateful for what this experience was teaching and strengthening in me. It was as if I was facing an old memory in order to be free of it, as if I had been given a moment to re-choose. As a child, I had chosen the comfort of approval; as an adult, I was choosing the discomfort of freedom. As I continued the conference, a new steeliness grew within me – I felt as if I had finally grown up!

As it turned out, I later learned that the woman with the cold eyes was furious because the sound system was interfering with her hearing aid and she had to leave each session because the irritation in her ears became too much. The rolling of the eyes and the walking out of the room had nothing to do with me.

While this happened quite a few years ago, the experience was very significant in terms of departing from old scripts of the past.

Releasing the past from the present

When patterns repeat themselves, they may be giving us a second chance to depart from and transform past experiences. They may be asking us to choose between the past and the present, between placing our value on other people's approval or the freedom of being authentic. We like to think we are totally in charge of our own lives, but we are frequently driven and shaped by old scripts; we are often determined by mental processes and old maps from our early lives. While we might no longer be that frightened child, we may continue to act from the same script that we acted from in the past. You know the scene:

you scan a room, looking for the disapproving face. You try to figure out how to change yourself in order to get a nicer response. You might start placating, trying to impress, arguing with, disappearing or doing whatever the old script drives you to do. When this happens, you are being automated by what psychology refers to as old 'internal working models'. Facing these internal processes is not easy, but through awareness you can gradually become more liberated from repeating the same patterns over and over again. You might have to excavate a few malevolent monsters, perhaps some from your schooldays; bullies in the schoolyard, goody-goody classmates, nit-picking teachers etc. They may have long departed, but are still lurking as the critic inside our subconscious. They may still be there, leaching our energy, disparaging us, ridiculing us, dismissing us, telling us we are no good or not very intelligent. We need to have a bit of fun here (those historic figures will never find out) so, how about you let yourself give vent – start trashing them, let rip, kill them off, bury them alive or draw ridiculous cartoons of them where they are smaller than in reality. (I placed big goofy glasses on the nose of my bully, which, of course, I covered with gruesome acne!) By saying a resolute 'no' to their historical but internal shaming voices, you begin to say 'yes' to a bigger you and a bigger life.

Viktor E. Frankl, a survivor of the Nazi concentration camps, espoused an inspiring inner freedom in the face of adversity. In *Man's Search For Meaning* he says, 'Everything can be taken from a man but one thing; the last of the human freedoms – to choose one's attitude in any given set of circumstances, to choose one's own way.'[22] He, himself had discovered an inner strength, so much so that even when the torturers tried to destroy him, he discovered that he actually had more freedom than the torturers themselves. 'Every day, every hour, offered the opportunity to make a decision, a decision which determined whether you would or would not submit to those powers which threatened to rob you of your very self, your inner freedom ... '.[23] Frankl said he was able retain his integrity and his power to choose a response. In fact, the freedom he discovered has become the cornerstone of many present-day leadership-training courses.

The process of choosing to grow is often called the 'journey of individuation', a concept coined by psychologist Carl Jung. He tells us: 'To the extent that a man is untrue to the law of his being and does not rise to personality, he has failed to realise his life's meaning. Fortunately, in her kindness and patience, nature never puts the fatal question as to the meaning of their lives into the mouths of most people. And where no one asks, no one need answer.'[24] If we are 'untrue to the law of our being', we cannot grow into that unique version of ourselves that we are meant to become.

Integral to the process of individuation is the reintegration of those parts of ourselves from which we have been estranged; it is a re-welcoming of the forgotten parts of us – the poor, the lame, the blind (Lk 14: 13).

Timmy

One leg dragging behind him, he wandered the streets in a faded grey jacket and shabby pants barely reaching his ankles. He was always alone, day and night, a bag slung over his shoulder; you would meet Timmy greeting you with that familiar grin through his stained, gapped teeth. He seemed to be everywhere, yet he was nowhere, uninvited and barging into conversations. 'Did you hear that I am going for the priesthood?' he would say. He would then desperately try to explain; his jaw would move but no words could come out, and during the long pauses his piercing eyes would seem to say, 'Don't give up on me'. By the time the next few words came out, people had either finished his sentence for him or had even walked away. No respecter of boundaries, Timmy's specialty seemed to be courting couples – yes, he would be right there in the middle, pleading to belong. The eczema, the dandruff on his collar, the stale smell, all made it difficult to include him and so, often excluded, he pottered away like a hurt, banished puppy. People often pretended not to see him and crossed the street. My last memory of him was of him holding out a fist of money, saying, 'I have the deposit for the Taizé trip.' My stomach felt a bit too delicate that day and the whiff from his breath and the food between his teeth was all a bit too much. 'No hurry with the money, Timmy,' I said. 'Sure, there's plenty of time, I'll take it from you the next time we meet.' There was no next time and no Taizé trip – the lonely figure wandering the streets was no more; the cold river took Timmy from us.

Some people said that Timmy was 'not all there'; unfortunately for Timmy, he was fully there. He was fully 'tuned in', so he felt every blow of rejection from the imprisonment of his disfigured face and indistinct speech. Perhaps Timmy was the suffering Christ in our midst: 'Without beauty, without majesty we saw him, no looks to attract our eyes; a thing despised and rejected by men, a man of sorrows and familiar with suffering, a man to make people screen their faces' (Is 53: 2–3). I hope he has finally put down the bag and taken off the grey coat; maybe he is now a priest for ever in the kingdom. No, I hope he is a bishop, or better still the patron saint of courting couples on street corners! And, Timmy, I hope you will hear my confession some day and that you will absolve me for the times you were lonely and I did not hear you, 'imprisoned' and I didn't see you, hungry to belong and I didn't include you.

People can be sent into our path to challenge our own 'disabilities', the parts we have turned away from. Often we turn away from a particular weakness in another because it mirrors a similar weakness in ourselves. Our ego doesn't like to see; it wants to remain blind. It can be liberating to discover that inside your own psyche, you are the one who is doing the rejecting, and you are also the one who is being rejected.

Really?

Yes, the egotistic, idealised self, with its impossible standards, is always criticising, despising and barraging the weak or the 'not good enough' you. Instead of turning away and splitting from our 'weaker' selves, we must find self-compassion and self-acceptance. Only then can we be present to others in their weakness. In naming our own fear of rejection, we become a little freer of the prison of the false self. 'The fear of rejection is the most dominant fear in all of human existence because it strikes against our most powerful and deepest need – the need for love, acceptance, affection and approval.'[25] In meeting people like Timmy and those whose 'dominant fear' is externally obvious, we are exposed to our own deepest need for 'love, acceptance, affection and approval'. There are two types of suffering: the pain of avoidance, which keeps us stuck, and the pain of facing, which sets us free. Maybe it is better therefore to watch carefully when we reject or turn away from a trait in another, because, as a friend of mine constantly reminds me, 'If you spot it, you got it'!

Brave hearts

Real heroes are those who do not seek to be such. Like the prophets of old, they know their own weaknesses and often prefer to be anonymous, but the universe calls them to step out from the crowd and into the arena.

The courageous are those who follow their hearts even while beset with vulnerability and hammering with terror. We desperately need people like this, especially leaders who are heroic in spirit; those who have a love of truth and so try to move beyond the fears of the ego. They say the difficult thing, not for the sake of being popular, but for the sake of the overall good of common humanity.

We sometimes picture heroes as gutsy, hell-bent on conquering, winning and emerging victorious. We can confuse bravery with 'doggedness', which is more a pushing of ourselves to be superhuman, becoming godlike in rising above our humanity (where just one innocuous comment can send us into freefall). Heroes are not those who go it alone; they are not the 'know-alls' who are always in charge. The real change-makers are those who rise and fall, and yet a phoenix keeps emerging out of the ashes of their failures and mistakes.

Heroes can say 'I don't know', and so give permission to the rest of us to admit that we don't know either (especially when we are pretending that we *do* know!). I am fortunate in that I meet some heroic people every day – I am not naming each of you now, but you know who you are! Here is why I see you as heroes:

You say the difficult thing, even when others do not like it, and even when you are frightened. You do not shrink back from naming your truth, and you do not hide behind a tough veneer. You surrender to uncertainty, and so you are not enslaved to the need to be right. You do not lean on titles or positions, but on an authority that comes from the soul. Like myself, you often mess up, but you get back up and ask for help. You frequently laugh at yourself and, most important of all, you allow me to laugh with you!

Heroes tend to be both admired and opposed. They change the direction of the system and so can be intensely loved or intensely hated. Christ, on his hero's journey, knew fear and vulnerability and constantly faced adversity. Every daring risk he took activated the criticism of others; they were forever hoping for something to use against him. As his light grew stronger, the minds of those who opposed him became narrower; however, the more they opposed him, the more freedom he espoused. He remained psychologically free. His life teaches us about integrity and healthy boundaries.

Boundaries

We need to discern when, and with whom, we should share those things that deeply matter to us. We have all experienced something like this: you tell someone about a hope or a dream you have for your life and you notice their eyes getting misty as they gaze off into the future, imagining how they themselves could do it (or maybe even planning how to get there before you!). Alternatively, they might change the subject because they don't want to be reminded of those dreams and desires that they themselves have ignored.

The cattle in the field behind our house have chewed the young shoots of the garden hedge outside our kitchen window. The shoots were too young and tender to be without a fence around them. Likewise, we frequently allow ourselves and our dreams to be chewed up and spat out by real – or imagined – opposers.

It can be difficult for others to accept our boundaries, but it helps to remember that they may very well be benefactors later on when they receive something from our renewed and less co-dependent presence. In stepping back to discover and align ourselves with our values and our own soul voice, we become empowered to liberate others to find theirs.

Stepping on to the dance floor

In contrast with what many people believe, I do not think that putting ourselves 'out there' necessarily becomes easier with practice. Each time I am invited to give a talk (or when I start to write a book), my critic returns with full force; it gathers accusers around me, hurling critical missiles that go something like this: "Who does she think she is? She's making such an eejit of herself ... '. I even sometimes talk back to my imaginary opponents: 'Leave me alone, that's not fair, I'm not a spotlight grabber ... '. Sometimes I win the argument, sometimes they do, but either way, this toxic tango goes nowhere. Homesick for the comfort zone, I try to drum up a few excuses to prevent exposure: I will wait until I have it 'more together', when I have more energy, another qualification, when I feel more confident etc.

One eventually discovers the futility of netting applause; it not only weakens our own resolve and leverages us backwards, but it also betrays the source that entrusted us with the unique gift of simply being ourselves. Of course, we must be open to critical feedback, but only from those who are also prepared to be vulnerable, those who also risk exposure and who dare to be on the dance floor. Remember, the only people who are sufficiently qualified to offer feedback are those who are also learning and falling, those who, like yourself, would prefer to sit it out, but choose instead to risk being part of the dance. In choosing to dance, we risk exchanging popularity for authenticity, even if, in our awkward beginnings, we do not look so good to our bench-sitting critics. This is not a time to deliberate, it is a time to keep dancing, even while knee-high in fear!

You must decide to dance, even if you stumble and fall – and remember, you *will* stumble and fall! You do not always get to choose the time and place when the universe calls you out – as the song says, even when you 'get the choice to sit it out or dance, I hope you dance'. [26]

I hope you still feel small when you stand beside the ocean; whenever one door closes, I hope one more opens. Promise me that you'll give faith a fighting chance, and when you get the choice to sit it out or dance ... I hope you dance ... I hope you dance.

CHAPTER 6

The Belly of the Whale

In-between Places

The aroma of lilies filled the visitors' parlour. I offered a little curtsy to the large statue (I wasn't really sure who she was but she looked holy). The freshly polished floors looked immaculate; in the background was the barely audible humming of vespers. Then I saw them bobbing along in single file, heads down, clutching large, rattling rosary beads. I was new in the city and had decided to visit the enclosed sisters (secretly half-considering joining them at the time). I stood up straight as one of them approached: an elderly sister with a beautiful smile that filled her face. We chatted for a few moments, and I mentioned that I was curious about their life. She interrupted by asking what I was currently doing. She seemed particularly interested in my studies in psychology and psychotherapy. I presumed it was because she reckoned it would come in handy if I was to live in community, but suddenly she leaned in, looked around, leaned in again and whispered softly, 'From your study in psychology, would you ever tell me, do men go through the menopause?' Before I had time to attempt any reply, she continued, 'Our parish priest here ... well ... he has changed lately, he has recently bought a motorbike and is riding around in leathers and a newly grown beard.' She lowered her tone, drew in a little closer, narrowed her eyes and whispered in a hushed tone, 'I am worried, you see, I think he might be ... suffering from ... *the change.*' When I looked confused, she said, 'Well, you know what I mean ... the menopause.' She then drew forth from her deep pocket a crinkled prayer, handed it to me and asked that maybe I would say it for him; so that, she explained, 'he might get better soon'. She continued to ask questions about various symptoms of mid-life crisis and seemed to forget all about my vocational crisis!

Mid-life

Mid-life is often the time when we take stock, when we realise that what sustained us at the dawn of our lives is no longer sufficient for the evening. It is a stage in life when we tend to become more reflective, where we begin to ask a different set of questions. So, whether it is buying a motorbike or simply discarding a few social norms, the unlived life can start to surface. Interestingly, it is also around the mid-life stage that people begin to seek therapy and engage in self-awareness courses. It is a time when the more existential themes look for an entry into our consciousness. This is often accompanied by an uninvited sense of our own mortality. In mid-life we may find ourselves becoming less concerned with the pursuit of material things or with the dopamine rush of gathering accolades or achievements. While we become less inflamed by the passionate and sometimes grandiose fires of youth, our creative energies do not die; they simply shift direction. No longer so concerned with the building up of our empires, we begin instead to focus more on the legacies we want to leave behind on departing from this universe. Consequently, it can be a time when some non-essentials are discarded, and we find ourselves throwing out those old uniforms of perfectionism and social respectability. These changes may come slowly, or sometimes they are prefaced by the screeching sound of a handbrake turn when we realise we are sleepwalking down a cul de sac.

Ageing is 'one of the ways the soul nudges itself into attention to the spiritual aspect of life'.[27] The ageing process draws us into deeper questions; it 'forces us to decide what is important in life'.[28] While there is usually an age bracket (some say fifty upwards) associated with such a transition, I think circumstances can push somebody into a life crisis at just about any age; early suffering can, for example, thrust a person into new inner landscapes. In transitional times we can be a bit like the Israelites of old, wandering in the desert before crossing the Red Sea and entering into the Promised Land. While wandering in the desert of transitional times, we begin to ask questions that others may have the luxury of postponing. Such questions can come sharply into view whenever there is a collapse of some previous sources of security or identity. We begin to ask: Am I living what I proclaim? Do I find myself selling out on my values? Am I going through the motions by sticking to numbing routines that constantly exhaust me? Am I weary of people needing me only for my role, or for what I can produce? Are my own needs being ignored?

While our lives may appear unchanged externally, these questions can bring a whole shift of orientation in our inner landscapes. Of course, there are those who can continue, for a lifetime, to rail against any change; they manage to stay at the superficial without ever entering a time of transition.

Integration

The Latin word for 'integrate' is *integrare*, which means 'to make whole'. The more we embrace the less squeaky clean parts of ourselves, the less shocked we will be when they greet us unexpectedly. When we become friends with our 'shadow self' it is less likely to sneak out in inappropriate places (the shadow self is that part of us that we don't want the world to see; it is the part we have sent into exile). Much of how we function and relate is affected by processes below the radar of our conscious mind. We liberate ourselves, therefore, by choosing an *approach* strategy instead of an *avoidance* strategy.

Uncovering the shadow is a gradual process, but one in which we begin to unearth some precious treasures. We might discover that the shadowy places, when integrated, can become cornerstones on our journey. Psychologist Carl Jung considered the shadow side to be 90 per cent gold, and suggested that integrating material from the shadow brings gifts into our lives. Franciscan Richard Rohr says: 'When all of you is there, you will know. When all of you is present, the banquet will begin.'[29]

My husband, Pat, was waiting for me in the car as some of the ladies who had participated in my retreat passed by. 'Wasn't she wonderful?' one of them commented. 'Yes,' said the other woman, 'and so gentle'. Pat, on hearing these comments, rolled his eyes to Heaven. I got into the car and took the bottle of juice from the front. I opened it and suddenly it fizzed up over the top of the bottle and onto my pristine jacket. 'Aw, f**k!' I shrieked, and let out a few more rather unrepeatable exclamations. Pat started the engine, smirking to himself, while muttering, 'Yeah, she's so gentle'. After a while I laughed too – although I had a sneaking suspicion that he had maliciously shaken up the bottle beforehand! Maybe he did it to 'shake up' any notions I might have about being 'all light' in my new-found 'angel complex'. Being 'all light' is just as dangerous as being all dark, because what is pushed into the dark is savagely waiting to erupt. Yes, the banquet begins when all the parts are allowed to be present. The dark and light need to be allowed to sit peacefully alongside one another, otherwise an internal civil war continues, in what can feel like 'a terrible contraction at our core'.[30]

Any person who chooses to grow will, at some time, enter into this transformative time of facing the shadow: 'The darkness of unconsciousness is very strong, but the light of awareness pushes it back. In Jung's morality of awareness, the struggle for individualism is a struggle for light, a struggle to get conscious, to get more of your experience and personality out of the dark so it can be respected, loved, accepted, and affirmed. The challenge is in relating consciously to the depth and complexity of who you are.'[31] In the process of 'getting more of your experience and personality out of the dark', you have to enter into it, into a place where you are transitioning between light and shadow.

A sneaky shadow
Even their designer sunglasses matched. They sipped the champagne with a certain poise, displaying their matching designer wedding rings. They exchanged nods and smiles. I looked at them thinking how great it must be always to look so perfectly presented to the world.

After a while, the woman excused herself from the table and walked the perfect catwalk towards the toilets. (I thought perfect people like them didn't even *need* to go to the toilet!) Her husband continued to sip his champagne and to eat his meal. Suddenly his fork fell onto the floor. He leaned down to pick it up. When he picked up the fork, he glared at it with slight disgust, looked around, leaned across and (horror of horrors) sneakily placed the *soiled* fork by his wife's plate! In exchange, he took her unused, gleaming fork and proceeded to eat his meal. After a while she returned, they clinked glasses and resumed their perfectly coordinated nods and smiles as she unknowingly placed a manky fork in her mouth!

Across the way, a few of us sat (hiding our laughter behind our 'early bird' menus). I whispered, 'Obviously, he couldn't give a fork.' That started us off again. 'Sneaky little fart', another one at our table muttered!

After a while the designer couple picked up their matching bags and, hand in hand, passed our table, leaving behind the whiff of an overpowering expensive perfume. Then, there was a strange noise ... What was that? Surely not a sneaky little release of flatulence? We looked at one another, all thinking the same thing again, 'sneaky little f ... ', and burst out laughing.

The dark side will always emerge in the sneakiest of ways. 'The dark side is actually a natural result of human development. It is filled with those inner urges, compulsions and dysfunctions of our personality that often go unexamined or remain unknown to us until we experience an emotional explosion or some other significant problem that causes us to search for a reason. At times the dark side seems to leap on us unexpectedly, but in reality it has slowly crept up on us ... it has been a lifetime in the making. [32]

A slip of the tongue (or a slip of the fork) can be a 'lifetime in the making'. Maybe it is better to face the discomfort of our shadow or repressed anger rather than transfer it into couple sadism!

A whale of a time

The Book of Jonah tells of one of the minor prophets in the Bible: a Hebrew prophet named Jonah, son of Amittai. The biblical story gives an account of God instructing Jonah to go to the city of Nineveh, to prophesy its impending destruction. Jonah tries to escape his divine mission, but a powerful storm arises and he is swallowed by a huge whale. He remains in the whale's stomach for three days and three nights, until eventually he is spat out onto the beach and goes on to answer the call in a renewed way. In mythology, 'the belly of the whale' is described by Joseph Campbell as a transitional time that occurs after crossing a threshold where there is no turning back: 'The idea that the passage of the magical threshold is a transit into a sphere of rebirth is symbolised in the worldwide womb image of the belly of the whale.' [33] Here we might have to wrestle with hidden gulfs of violence, seething impulses below the surface.

> *Here one can neither stand nor lie nor sit*
> *There is not even silence in the mountains*
> *But dry sterile thunder without rain*
> *There is not even solitude in the mountains,*
> *But red sullen faces sneer and snarl*
> *From doors of mud cracked houses* [34]
> – T. S. ELIOT

In mythology, when the hero crosses the threshold, he often comes to the edge of a dangerous place, sometimes underground, often a dark cavern that can be symbolic of the unconscious. In many fairy tales and myths there is often a journey into a cave. Interestingly, the Sanskrit word *guha* means both heart and cave. A journey to a cave is often an archetypal symbol of a journey to the heart, the cave being considered as the place of rebirth. In ancient Greece, people entered caves to be reborn. We are reminded here of the death and resurrection of Jesus, three days and three nights, time spent in the tomb before resurrecting into new life.

A necessary struggle
Only when we face the complexity of our dark night can we begin to shine a light into the dark places of our outer

world. Whether we call our experience a mid-life crisis or a breakdown, the time we spend in the whale's belly can be a type of rebirth, rather like a 'boot camp' for the soul!

In winter, bears are known to seek out dark and hidden caves where they find warmth and safety for their sleep through the long winter months. Likewise, the seed remains underground in winter, growing in silence and darkness. All the beauty and creativity of the flower is in the seed, but it needs this time under the earth, a period of gestation, until its time of emerging. There are also seeds hidden and buried in our hearts; they too need time for germinating.

There is a story of a young girl who noticed a butterfly trying to emerge from its chrysalis. Struggling mightily, it tried to push itself through the small opening. In sympathy, the girl snipped the cocoon, giving ample room for the butterfly to come through. It quickly emerged but its body was swollen and it crawled around on its belly. The poor butterfly could not fly. The little girl, without knowing it, had interrupted the natural unfolding of its wings. The butterfly did not go through the necessary transformative process whereby its wings, drawing fluid from its body, could unfold.

How terrifying it must be for the caterpillar to surrender itself and dissolve into something else, not knowing what new form it will take. In dying to its old form, it does not yet know that it will become a beautiful butterfly. We too are afraid of surrendering to this process of transformation. It might help to remember that our lives are a chrysalis where we are always being called to something new, a new stage of evolving.

Sometimes, like Jonah in the belly of the whale, which represents the lowest point of the journey, we have to wait, in this dark, lost, directionless place. Maybe there is a place called 'lost' that is actually a necessary stage on the journey. This waiting stage can be a most discerning and reflective time. Sometimes, even times of depression can actually be creative times – a season of darkness where something is dying and something is being born. We can, therefore, do a disservice by telling somebody who is depressed to 'pull themselves together', because maybe it is their time to enter the 'belly of the whale'. Eventually, like Jonah, they may be spat out onto some new ground. In hindsight they may see the necessity of the waiting time, perhaps even the necessity of the depression. On recognising a new inner resource, they may even be thankful for what certainly didn't feel like having a whale of a time!

CHAPTER 7

Fly or Die

Understanding our Fears

With my foot on an imaginary brake pedal, knuckles white, I kept asking, 'How much longer?' The turbulence had already gone on for more than fifteen minutes. 'Please keep your seatbelts fastened and avoid using the toilets.' The cabin crew announcer's voice grated on me. What does it matter if you are sitting on the loo while going down over the Atlantic Ocean? I mean, would you really care at that stage if you are caught showing your bum to the world with your pants down around your ankles? The 'bottom' would have fallen out of your world by then anyway! With dry mouth and sweaty palms, I tried to calm myself by turning to the person next to me and attempting to make small talk. Bad decision! 'Terrible about the plane that went down over Russia,' she said. My heart hammered. 'Yeah, it was terrible all right,' I said (pretending to know what she was talking about in the hope that she wouldn't continue). She went on, 'And apparently it just dismantled in mid-air and ... '. That was it – something snapped inside, my mind whirred, 'Get me out of here, fast.' I suddenly realised that 'getting out' was an even worse prospect. The words of the Billy Joel song blared in my head: 'Yes, we would all go down together ... '!

A picture unfolded before me whereby we are all swirling through the air, hand luggage going down over the Atlantic. Some passengers are still sitting in flying seats; the cabin crew are now off their trollies; other passengers are hanging on to the seat of their pants while sitting on the loo! My thoughts are suddenly interrupted again by the intercom. 'We will be preparing to descend shortly. Please return your seats to the upright position and make sure your seatbelts are securely fastened. Do not use the toilets ... '. Here she goes again, obsessing about the loo, and besides what use are seatbelts if the plane is dismantling ... ? The song continues in my head. 'We would all go down together ... '. Suddenly, the pilot speaks; he makes some announcement about the weather and how it is raining in Cork. Who cares about the weather, sure getting wet won't matter when we are dead ... suddenly, it dawns on me: did he say *Cork*? The song stops playing in my mind, all is quiet – we are landing, arriving on solid ground ... I can breathe again, my mouth feels moist again. I turn to the person next to me and say, 'Nice meeting you,' as genuinely as I can manage.

Fight or flight

We are evolutionarily hardwired to watch for threats rather than opportunities. Every human being and every animal has this survival instinct. In avoiding 'danger', we often stay in the comfort zone, because staying 'safe' is very important to the amygdala part of the brain. The amygdala is a bit like the night security in the hotel – its job is to keep an eye on things and to watch out for danger. The amygdala stores old memories, which get activated instantly whenever there appears to be any threat. Panicky thoughts activate the amygdala, which cause the 'fight or flight' response to kick in, regardless of whether the fear is real or imagined. Following this, adrenaline is released, the heart rate increases, cortisol moves through the body, blood is drawn towards the muscles, perspiration increases and digestion slows down.

Needless to say, it is very difficult to process any logical thought or wisdom while you are being bombarded by all this anxious reactivity.

When we are afraid, we tend to stick to what we think is reliable. In this fixed mindset we do not stretch ourselves or test our boundaries. When, however, we take risks for the sake of change and growth, we are operating from a 'growth' mindset.

Fly or die
The television documentary was showing how a little bird was learning to fly: how it is pushed from the nest by the mother, who then waits to scoop up the little bird so that it finds its own wings. It appeared to me as if the

mother was coaxing it. 'Come on, little bird, come to mommy, you are nearly there.' All the while I was saying (as I clung to my seat, pulling the cushions protectively around me), 'Don't do it, birdie, it's a bad world out there, go back to bed, you might fall, better the devil you know ... '. The more the mother coaxed the little bird, the louder I shrieked, 'No, don't do it ... you'll get your death of cold out there, you don't even have a cap or coat ... '. Mother bird continued to call her baby out. I shuddered at that image, because, like most of us, I know something of that fear of falling and fear of failing, fear of letting go – that frightening descent into an unknown space. I found myself saying to the little bird, 'Hang on to your nest, baby, better be safe than sorry, you cannot be too careful nowadays, good nests are hard to come by.' All the while the mother is circling around her young with food in her mouth. She is luring the little bird, who eventually falls into the air. Oh, this is cruel, I think (as I curl my legs under me on the sofa, stuff another bit of chocolate into my mouth and draw the soft velvet throw around me). The little bird is now in freefall, tumbling through the air, until something starts to happen: it discovers it has wings!

I never liked hearing how little birds learn to fly. I am not really an adventurous person, more the nest type. I am always looking for nests and find it difficult to leave them. Why do we cling to safety and deny ourselves the freedom that our hearts long for? When we get used to feeling a constriction, it can be rather terrifying to embrace freedom and all the uncertainty that can come with it. Most of us have developed unconscious protective patterns in order to defend ourselves from sudden exposure. When we come up against any new risk, these patterns are challenged and we shrink back, even though we know deep down that real life and real freedom can only be ours when we leave our comfort zone. The real change-makers leave their nests in order to access a perspective that cannot be gleaned from confined spaces. Living near the edge is both terrifying and exciting. Celtic monks lived near the edge; the desert dwellers of the early Church lived near the edge. I know of a writer and poet who sold her rather large house and her belongings to live in a very simple cottage near the edge of the ocean. She explained that she is more inspired 'at the edge'. Life continually asks us to move out a little bit from the nest and risk edgy places.

It is time to leave your nest, a spirit called 'freedom' whispered.

Ah no, not yet, I am too afraid, I answer, as I see the sheer fall of precipice underneath.

It is time to leave your nest, whispered another spirit called 'joy'.

Ah no, not now, I am not ready, it is cold out there, I am only a child, protests a tiny, frightened internal voice.

Do not say you are only a child. I will give you wings,

I will make you great. Go now, I will be the very air that supports you, a voice called 'courage' calls as she soars and dives around my heart.

But, what if ... what if there is nothing? I ask, peering over the prison wall of my ego nest.

How do I know that I won't fall into an abyss?

The spirit replies, *It is time, a new kingdom is close at hand; you must leave this place, this limited outgrown nest. Look at the great beyond.*

I take a peek, I draw back ... Something pushes me, the husk around my heart dismantles, and I tumble internally. Terrified, I fall through an unfamiliar air in my mind. I descend through layers of safety mechanisms, masks, neuroses, plummeting deeper and deeper through my defences, until I feel something I never felt before – the power of my breath and my soul wings!

Empty nest syndrome

When we cling to our little nests, we can become very self-obsessed, suspicious, competitive (sometimes secretly hoping that our nest is bigger and better, more secure, and with better insulation!) We compete and fear that someone else might have a bigger, posher, more exclusive nest in a better location (or perhaps like the swallows, a second nest abroad somewhere!). We might redecorate and add extensions to our nests but continue to trade all our inheritance of freedom for this tiny, restrictive psychological nest! Inside our nest, we have the illusion of being safe, and so we are afraid that beyond our little controlled world, there may be nothing; we fear we may freefall into an abyss, into nothingness. Being human, we fear annihilation, those places where we imagine we could lose all that we are, or more accurately, all that we *think* we are. Paradoxically, it is when we have lost our external or constructed 'safety' that we often feel authentically safe. It is often when we find ourselves tumbling into an abyss that we discover something deeper is holding us; it is as if there are invisible arms waiting to catch us. It is only then we know what 'home' really feels like. We are able to say, with the psalmist: 'If I come to the end, I am still with you' (Ps 139: 18).

There comes a time in all our lives when we know we will die a little inside if we do not leave some of our old familiar nests, especially those husks and roles of our false self. This leaving of the familiar starts when we leave the safety of the womb to enter into the unknown experiences of earthly life. Many other leavetakings follow, right through from childhood to adulthood.

Like the young bird, we too discover a larger and more expansive vista when we leave the tiny containers of our safe nests. We find a larger place of belonging when we discover that our true home is in the whole boundless universe, that infinite source which, amazingly, also resides in the deepest core of our being. Mother bird, our Universal Mother, knows that even while we keep clinging to our nests, our spirits long to soar. She waits patiently, 'like an eagle watching its nest, hovering over its young' (Dt 32: 11–2).

Something bigger than the ego-self is waiting to catch us when we fall. We see others waiting for us, those who themselves had the courage to let go, those who also left behind some old nests. Exhilarated with a new freedom we are now celebrating the wind beneath our wings. In losing our nests, we find our wings; in losing life, we find life.

Dance in a moveable nest

I came off the phone, satisfied with how many people I had contacted to advise them about the dangerous weather that had been forecast. 'Stay inside,' I warned. 'Stay safe, do not venture out. Footpaths are slippery, you could fall.' I cancelled my own New Year celebration plans, threw another block on the fire and heaved a sigh of relief ... Ah, everyone is safe now, a great excuse for a night by the fire and a comforting cup of tea. I went to put the kettle on and suddenly I tumbled over my untied shoelace – and what a tumble! I fractured my ribs and bruised my eye socket. I writhed in pain for the next couple of days, seething to myself while hearing about the exploits of those who had a great night out, dancing and ringing in the New Year (the ones that ignored my warnings about falling and hurting themselves!).

Staying in the 'safe nest' does not guarantee we will not fall; in fact, what we *think* is keeping us safe can be the most unsafe place, spiritually and psychologically. Paradoxically, we can find real freedom only when we seek our *internal security amidst external insecurities*. In trying to prevent ourselves falling, and in securing all the external conditions, we might be doing the very thing that 'trips us up'.

Psychoanalyst and paediatrician Donald Woods Winnicott (1896–1971) developed the concept of 'the container', something he describes as a holding environment offered by the mother to her infant. This safe container is laid down by the loving care of the mother and is something the infant needs for building a strong sense of self. If, as children, we did not internalise any real inner sense of safety, we were most likely left experiencing the world as an unsafe place. Consequently, a deficit in this secure base can, in later life, result in us desperately clinging to numerous outer securities and certainties. We do this in an attempt to protect ourselves against the perceived, sometimes real dangers of the world.

Outgrown nests
Jane sacrificed her career in order to care for her parents. She gave up her hobbies and social life and rarely went out with friends, yet she frequently complained that others were having a good time while she felt stuck at

home. When people offered her a break, she thanked them politely but said her parents would find it difficult to adjust to anyone except herself taking care of them. She was often in a low mood; a type of depression emanated from her, which she dismissed as tiredness from not having any break. She was frequently praised by others for her sacrifice; this affirmation gave her some semblance of self-worth. Eventually her parents died, and everyone hoped that Jane would now find her freedom, but while the external confinement was gone, the internal one remained. After her parents died, Jane began to die inside. She drifted from one day to the next, feeling as if life had no meaning, and besides, she said, it was 'too late now to start a career or start socialising'.

Jane had hidden behind the caretaking of her parents. It was only after fighting constant exhaustion and prolonged depression that she eventually became aware that she, in fact, had needed her parents more than they had needed her. She had stayed inside a comfort zone, a safe nest, while deep down she was terrified of embracing her own life.

Health or safety?

While it is highly admirable that somebody would give up her own life to care for a parent, it is also necessary to look at whether this is done in freedom or out of some inability to detach. Leavetaking is necessary for spiritual and emotional well-being. Trying to stay safe can be the unhealthiest option for the soul. Perhaps that is why Jesus said, 'You must leave father and mother' (Lk 14: 26). This, of course, does not mean that we neglect to care for our parents; in fact, 'father and mother' might have been deceased for many years but psychologically we still have not left them. We might be rebelling against them but still remain enmeshed, so whether we continue to attach, idealise or even resent them, we might still not have 'left father and mother'. Life invites us towards many leavetakings – not just those in relation to our biological parents, but also in regard to those outgrown family scripts, secrets or rules, as well as those stale allegiances to cultural beliefs and ideologies.

When we cling fearfully to our containers and their illusory images of safety, when we cling to the known and mistrust the unknown, everything outside the confines of the container seems very frightening, every loss feels overwhelming. We can turn our jobs, our caretaking, our institutions, our relationships, our religion and our positions into carefully constructed nests. Unfortunately, such strategies will not bring us the safety we crave. Like the mother bird coaxing her chick to put trust in its wings (rather than in its nest), we must coax ourselves to develop new inner resources to cope with the unpredictability and insecurities of our outer lives. We must develop a character structure with an inbuilt sense of safety; otherwise we shrink inside and shut ourselves down against life whenever some new challenge beckons.

Nesting prayers

Paddy, an elderly relative, had lived a prayerful life, but his uppermost prayer was in relation to his own death. He lit candles every evening and asked for a happy death – he asked that he be 'spared suffering'. He was so obsessed with praying for his death that he forgot to live his life! His prayers asked that he be spared from losing independence, and his dread was that he would have to depend on anybody. 'A happy death' meant just God and Paddy, and no 'intruders' (which was how Paddy described anyone who interrupted his isolation). He carefully orchestrated his life whereby everything he did was tried and tested and guaranteed not to fail, guaranteed to keep him safe. Paddy had been separated from his mother at birth and all of his life he was unconsciously 'looking for mother', looking for a secure base. Paddy's prayers were answered – he *did* have a happy death, though not as he visualised it and certainly not 'spared of suffering'. He had to face his dreaded dependence on others; he needed to be cared for, fed, washed and all the things he prayed 'would never happen'. Surprisingly, he was psychologically and spiritually set free by being pushed from his nest of self-reliance to a place where he had to trust the 'intruders' – the community of humanity – that held him until mother-death swooped him up into her eternal embrace.

Afraid to leave, afraid to stay

We often pray to a God that will keep us safe, protected, guarded, yet at the same time we long for adventure, growth and new life. Frequently we are begging God that something will not happen whereby we are thrown out of our comfort zones, yet grace is often experienced through facing the very thing we have been fighting against. If we do not feel safe in our bodies and in the world, we will have great difficulty in letting go of anything familiar (even if it is not good for us). Sigmund Freud suggested that all our present-day experiences of fear and anxiety reproduce the feelings of that first separation from our mothers. Our early attachment (or its lack) to our mothers or primary carers is a huge factor around our ability to let go and embrace change: 'As a young child, you needed to connect in order to move forward. As an infant, you depended on your mother to give the nourishment you needed, and your attention focused almost exclusively on that relationship. When you were a toddler, she became a background object as you began to develop and function more independently.'[35]

CHAPTER 8

Mammy

Cutting the Umbilical Cord

She swished the frothy milk, occasionally checking that it was lukewarm. She held the bucket firmly as the calves drank greedily, biting her delicate but worn hands. They swished their tails occasionally as they head-butted the buckets, draining every last bit of nourishment. They stole her from me, aggressively draining every last drop, dribbling their slippery saliva onto her apron. As she held the empty bucket, wisps of hair falling over her perspiring face, the best of her was taken; she had poured herself out. Leaning against the door, I stared at her stained overcoat, the one with the cold buttons. My mind began counting the hours, the minutes, longing for the moment when she would put on her 'mammy cardigan', the one with the safety pins and medals, and she would be indoors again. How much longer before the day would close, and the late evening silence would descend? How much longer until the milking would be finished and the cows would leisurely graze, their day's work done? How much longer? The annoying cat, now clawing at the milk buckets, seemed to ask the same question. Then the sun would cast its final soft light over the farmyard, the birds would say their vespers, the wellingtons would finally be removed and the furry chequered slippers taken from near the range; then the clinking of cups would begin. As the kettle purred on the hob, she would cut her home-made bread, cover it with thick butter and golden syrup, make hot sweet tea and she would finally be – Mammy.

Upsetting the 'apple tart'

'Mum', 'Mommy' or 'Mammy' is the first word most of us say and, at some level, it lies forever in our psyches, like a slice of warm apple tart. The word 'mammy' is like a cup of tea on a cold day, an extra blanket on a frosty night. While 'mammy' can be like a hammock to collapse into, a shelter from the storm, it can also be the most evocative word for our other hidden impulses, such as rage and grief. There is no doubt that to honour one's mother is one of the highest virtues. Many feel they would dishonour the Great Mother archetype by even thinking of the pain or grief associated with wounded mothering; that it would be blasphemous to speak 'negatively' of the infallible mother. The mother archetype occupies a powerful space, not just in our individual unconscious, but also in our collective unconscious. While there are many universal underlying archetypal images, the

'Irish mother' has its own primordial features; it can be associated with the keeping up of appearances, with family secrets etc. It may feel disloyal to admit any weaknesses in our experiences of mother. Consequently, we can remain in denial about the truth of our own story and the truth of the generational line of mothers that perhaps needs to come to light for healing. Paradoxically, it is this 'bringing into the light' that not only sets us free, but in some way also sets free our mothers, and perhaps the whole lineage of mothers. We might be afraid of losing our 'perfect mother' image if we explore the full array of our feelings; we may be afraid to 'upset the apple tart'.

The mother wound

Every mother wants to provide her child with the basic ingredients for building his or her foundation. She knows instinctively that if the baby can rest with mother, it can rest in its own nature. She knows that this is crucial to the baby's development, giving it a sense of its own being, without which it would rely on a false self to get a sense of existence: 'It is in large part the stimulation of his skin by touch which enables the child to emerge from his own skin.'[36] The deprivation of physical contact is very painful because, without it, physiological systems do not function properly; even the growth of the brain is affected by the amount of touch we receive in the early stages of life. The development of the self takes place through the mother-child bond: 'Mother's non-demanding presence makes the experience of formlessness and comfortable solitude possible, and this capacity becomes a central feature in the development of a stable and personal self.'[37] Without 'mother's non-demanding presence', we retain a sense of non-belonging, a feeling of homelessness or a perpetual fear of abandonment. We might try to 'change' these feelings with cognitive gymnastics, positive thinking, medication and so on, until we eventually acknowledge the mother wound. If, however, we continue to sanitise, sanctify and idealise our mother while demonising ourselves, we will feel very dissociated in our adult lives. While all our wounding certainly cannot be put down to mothering wounds, psychological research clearly demonstrates the extent to which a deficit in mothering affects every area of our lives. If we are to heal, we have to acknowledge this deficit, and connect with it in a way that brings healing and integration. When we were children, we needed to have our mother in our sight, and we cried and threw tantrums when we could not see her. Whenever she would leave the room, the memory of her earlier presence did not console us in her absence. We were not able to say, 'Ah, sure, mommy is gone out to buy some groceries, I will wait here and enjoy my bottle and she will be back soon.' No, baby feels devastated; mommy is gone, that is all baby knows. Over time we learned how to internalise her presence and so drew a conclusion that when mommy leaves, she always returns; because it happened before, it will happen again. This is a crucial learning whereby we became sufficiently nourished by her presence that we were able to withstand times of absence. Gradually, there will be less need of her constant presence as the infant grows and takes more autonomous risks. The secure base is no longer experienced solely on the outside, but is actually now experienced within the self.

Rite of passage

Edward worked hard to build a facade of strength and resilience; he bolstered his sense of self in the world through his numerous achievements and successful enterprises. This worked pretty well – except whenever he asked a woman out on a date. He worked too hard at making an impression, while separating himself from the aspects of himself that he perceived would not gain approval.

Edward had never received adequate mirroring or connection from his mother, and so as an adult he tried to find connection by impressing, performing and proving. Essentially, he was begging for his sense of self instead of being present to who he was. The women that he was trying to impress would find his macho facade off-putting rather than attractive. He continued on this treadmill until eventually his exhausting macho compulsion was punctured when he befriended the mother wound. He had to gradually reconnect with the self he had estranged himself from for many years. This journey was like a rite of passage (something that was prevalent in earlier times, where young males underwent initiation rituals for transitioning from boyhood to manhood). 'Initiation taught the boy that there were more ways to deal with the world than by simply trying to fix, manage or control life around him. Initiation taught the male how to bow instead of strut before the Mystery at the heart of all life.'[38]

When Edward decided to bow rather than strut, the women around him began to react differently; when they no longer encountered his facade, some even fell in love with him!

The rite of passage is a central aspect of the hero's journey; it empowers us to cut ties with parental bondages and outdated scripts in order to cross the threshold into more mature living.

Attachment

Attachment theory indicates that it is most difficult to deal with or even acknowledge the mother wound when it occurs at a preverbal stage. It is a particularly complex healing process when mother was physically present and apparently functioning well, but was emotionally absent. We can, in such circumstances, feel it is our own fault for having needs. The child may have the feeling 'mother is not there'; this can be translated by the child to 'mother is not there because I'm not good enough' and, consequently, at an even more primitive level, 'I myself am not there either'. This prevents the infant being fully present in its own body and in its own world. There may have been a perceived abandonment, hurt or neglect, but even this perception has to be acknowledged, because it is the child's internal experience that matters in the context of healing.

Children can actually give up the wanting and deny their needs by disappearing inside themselves. To feel a longing that you perceive cannot be met is too painful and is therefore relegated to unconsciousness, where it goes out of awareness, only to resurface later on. The 'separation anxiety' creates ambivalence: the child may try to avoid attachment completely, or may cling desperately, or may sometimes vacillate from one extreme to the other. All are attempts to resolve the underground attachment wound.

We often continue to abandon ourselves emotionally in the same way as an earlier perceived, or real, emotional abandonment may have taken place. We may continue to negate our own needs if they were negated earlier in life: 'Severe separations in early life leave emotional scars on the brain because they assault the essential human connection; the mother-child bond which teaches us that we are loveable. We cannot be whole human beings

– indeed, we may find it hard to be human – without the sustenance of this first attachment.'[39]

Healing the mother wound

Many of us may have received a distorted reflection of ourselves through the eyes of the adult figures in our childhood; parents or caregivers may have looked at us through the filters of their own expectations and so we may have tried to be the person they hoped we would be. Instead of being children, we become 'little adults', thrust into roles and responsibilities created by dysfunction. This would have prevented us subtly from experiencing the full range of our own emotions and personality traits. As a result, there can remain in us a chronic shame around those 'prohibited' aspects of our personality. We would most likely close down and deem those parts of us to be off limits (which is like closing down our very souls).

I remember being very young and hearing my mother say, 'She is no burden, she is so quiet, sure you would not know if she were dead or alive.' I had learned that this burdened household could not hold the fullness of my personality, so I learned to 'play dead' and to disappear inside myself. It seemed a much safer option to just exit and check out than to remain present for all the vicissitudes and pain of my surroundings. I cleverly discovered a mechanism whereby I found a gallery seat (in my head) from which I observed the ring of fire! Up here, I could not get burned; I evaluated all of life, events and people, but avoided feeling part of it. I reckoned this was the best strategy, convincing myself that anyone you get close to will get sick, disappoint you and eventually die. I reckoned it would be rather foolish to get involved with something you ultimately cannot control. Because I could not create immunity from pain, neither for myself nor for those I loved, this gallery seat seemed the perfect solution. However, in adult life I discovered (rather painfully) how, in disconnecting from the suffering around me, I had disconnected from my own soul.

Checking out

When we escape into some fantasy world or deaden ourselves so we can't feel anything, we learn to dissociate. When we 'check out' like this, we become disconnected from the core of our being, removing ourselves from any need for close contact. Needless to say, this only serves to exacerbate our isolation.

We cannot heal what we cannot feel, therefore we have to begin by telling somebody the real story. Most importantly, we have to tell ourselves the real story. John Bradshaw, author and psychologist, calls this 'original pain work', which he says involves actually experiencing the original repressed feelings. He says, 'It is the only thing that will bring about "second-order change", the kind of deep change that truly resolves feelings.'[40]

This original pain work is similar to the process of bereavement, where we work through stages of disbelief, denial, anger etc. Everything that happened remains part of us, but healing mobilises the frozen energy where wounding once took place. In my experience of working with people, I have discovered that when the truth, no matter how difficult it is, is named, then the healing begins.

The world and its mother!

The first step in healing involves trust; you need to trust that others can help you heal, people with whom you can be truly honest, that you can ask for your needs to be met in honest ways. In this way you are mothering yourself with good boundaries and healthy self-care and learning to perceive yourself as competent, valuable and loveable. Every psychological process and every hero's journey necessitates that we leave mother, meaning that we cut the energy around the umbilical chord. This liberates us, and we begin to see her as the wonderful person that she was (or still is); we can see that she too was heroic. In gaining understanding and compassion for our own story, we begin to find compassion for our mother's story and therefore become more able to forgive any deficits in our relationship with her. We only truly let go and depart from this pain when we acknowledge that our mothers did the best they could, and we might even recognise that we ourselves also did the best we could.

PART THREE

Searching for Treasure

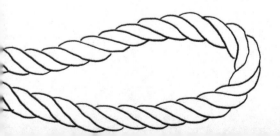

CHAPTER 9

Gifts in Unexpected Places

Breakthroughs from Breakdowns

'I don't care, it doesn't affect me, I'm tough, I'm bigger than this.' I kept repeating this to myself as I drove home from an event where I had bumped into a friend from whom I had been estranged for many years. During those years I had frequently reached out in an attempt at reconciliation, but it had not been reciprocated. I had managed to reconstruct my life, or at least gain a bit of distance from the loss, but now the wound had been gashed open again. Thoughts went to and fro in my head in constant loops: How dare she snub me like that? Why was I so stupid as to talk to her? My thoughts swung from blaming her to blaming myself and back again to blaming her! None of this alleviated the pain, so I began instead desperately reassuring myself how 'strong' I was and how much it was *not* affecting me. Head in the air, I stopped at the garage where I filled my diesel car – with petrol! And off I went again, radio blaring (so that I couldn't hear the pain in my heart), but soon I became aware of the protests of the car as it struggled to keep going. I had been steaming ahead into the horizon of my autonomous life when, bang – the car broke down in the middle of the busy motorway. Eventually, the man from breakdown assistance arrived to tow away the car. He must have spotted my embarrassment, and he said, 'Sure, it happens easily, especially when the mind is somewhere else.' The mind was indeed 'somewhere else', employed in fighting what was in my heart. Now, unable to keep steaming ahead, I had to befriend the pain under the 'I don't care strategy'. I had to admit to myself that I cared deeply and perhaps would continue to do so for the rest of my life. Strangely, on acknowledging this painful reality, my shoulders dropped and I took the first real breath that morning. In naming the pain, the intensity of it actually lessened; I was no longer pouring denial onto the wound (which had been as toxic as pouring petrol into the diesel tank). I discovered that I cannot heal what I refuse to feel.

In my desperate attempt to avoid the feelings of hurt, I employed the blame game. This pointing-the-finger strategy temporarily discharged the discomfort – until the breakdown. Then came the breakthrough, when I realised that I could not fix or change what happened with my head; instead I had to let it move through me. This moment of enlightenment softened the hard edges of my heart. It felt like a block of ice had started to melt under the warmth of some spiritual force. While the pain didn't magically go away, I somehow held it differently; it now occupies a different space in my heart and a different place in my life. It is no longer at 'the driving wheel'.

I really don't know how to define forgiveness, because just when we think we have forgiven, our hearts can freeze over again. However, when we hold the painful story in compassion, something softens and we let go a little; we even sometimes manage to see the other through the eyes of compassion (for a few minutes, anyway!). In contrast, when we choose not to forgive, we remain attached to our identity as 'the one who has been wronged'; we identify with being hurt to such a degree that we victimise ourselves. We become wounded over and over again as we replay the hurts in our mind. We may vacillate between blaming the other, or blaming ourselves, none of which brings freedom. Instead of engaging in mind games where we try to bolster ourselves, or endlessly try to justify our actions to ourselves, we can acknowledge the pain and begin to let go of the denial employed by our minds. Letting go is not a defeat, neither is it a condoning – rather it is dropping the fist, giving up the insistence that there must be a payback or a day of reckoning. This does not mean we are then freed from experiencing the pain or other residual feelings. Nevertheless, forgiveness may be the single greatest gift we can give ourselves; it is the decision to stop pouring toxic fuel into the engine of that which automates our lives.

Retribution or reconciliation

We often think that the hurt in our hearts can be resolved only by facing and having it out with the person who has hurt us, but this is not always possible, or even wise. Sometimes we will create further hurt for ourselves if the other person is not willing really to listen. It is especially difficult to forgive when the other person has closed any door to dialogue. In such a situation, you may have to release the relationship rather than try to restore it. You may have to accept that the other may continue to be in discord with you, and you may not be able to change that. Letting go of expectations for reconciliation is not easy, but is preferable to using up energy in continually planning and rehearsing all the things you might 'one day' say to someone. Eventually, you have to acknowledge that it is in fact your own life that is on hold for as long as you stay stuck at the scene of the crime. We might argue about why the other person 'deserves' our forgiveness when it is they who have done the hurting. We often think that by withholding our forgiveness we are somehow 'winning'. However, the act of forgiving is a gift to ourselves; it is a releasing of ourselves from unhealthy baggage. Hoping that we can change the other, or change the past, is a cul de sac. I often hear people say 'time is a great healer', but I think that is only partly true. Yes, time gives us distance from something, but a part of us can remain frozen for a lifetime, while still tethered to the one who has hurt us. Perhaps the only route to peace is through acknowledging that even though I may be unable to forget, I choose to forgive.

The human condition

Marie was sent to me for counselling. When somebody is 'sent' there can often be resistance at the beginning. Marie had truckloads of resistance. She sat on the chair, crossed her legs, folded her arms and narrowed her eyes. She looked at me suspiciously and said in a low but threatening tone, 'If you think I'm going to forgive my parents, you have another think coming.' She then sat back with a smirk of satisfaction. We hadn't even introduced ourselves, let alone had any discussion of her parents or forgiveness. Cautiously, I gradually established a relationship with her. Over the following weeks and months, we worked on her childhood issues. The armouring began very slowly to soften as the pain of her early experiences of neglect and abandonment began to tumble out. She sobbed cathartically as she once again felt the pain of the little girl she once was. On one occasion I was asking her about something that involved her parents, when her body language suddenly closed over and she glared at me. She stood up, raised her voice and said, 'Don't you dare blame my parents, you don't realise how much loss they had themselves when they were young, they couldn't do any better.' I was now moved to tears myself. What had been happening in those intervening months? Marie had forgiven her parents. While none of us had even mentioned the word forgiveness, by touching the pain of the child in her own heart, she somehow empathised and softened towards the little children that her mother and father had once been. She had connected with the only place where healing arises – the place of our common humanity. She re-crafted her story from that of victim to that of survivor. She faced her darkness, wrestled with her demons and emerged with a gift, a new empathy for herself, her parents and humanity. Marie made a true hero's journey.

A divine gift

The willingness to forgive is the most noble and heroic virtue of the human spirit. Most of the heroes that we admire had to dig deep in order to let go. We think of Nelson Mandela, who spent twenty-seven years in prison on Robben Island, and who is admired for his forgiving heart towards the apartheid regime in South Africa. We think of the resurrected body of Christ carrying the wounds of those who murdered him. We too carry wounds, but they do not have to define us. Rather than pointing the finger or shaking the fist, we can allow the heart to weep and we can eventually face life again, a little softer and a little wiser.

If we feel unable to extend forgiveness right now, we can show compassion to ourselves for not being able to forgive. That very act of compassion can open the heart. Who knows, we might meet one another in a time and place beyond the realm of who is right or who is wrong. We might then connect, no longer hurt to hurt, but heart to heart.

Releasing yourself – the sensitive soul

Are you one of us? Chances are that you may be, because there are a lot of us in the world; and besides, we read books like this! We are the ones who can feel tired from just breathing. We could say it was because we are so busy, so indispensable, but the truth is, it is because we are so bloody sensitive. I use the word 'bloody' intentionally here, because it does indeed bleed your soul when you are forever allowing life to leave its mark on you. If you are one of us, you will identify with some of the following. Our psyches are like rabbits, always on the alert, always 'full on', able to pick up all sorts of atmospheric vibes and passing vibrations. We easily, and frequently, skirt the edges of adrenalin burnout, and we soak up whatever 'lands' on us on any given day. Our minds are always playing chess games; negotiating the next move to stay ahead of the pain. We are all used up at the end of the day, yet we continue to 'work' through the night, mentally processing those residual energies left over from the day (not just our own but everybody else's too). When we do eventually go to sleep, our dreams play out scenes where we are nearly always the bad guy – at fault again! However, before you get out the violins and lament for us, we do have some good stuff. For example, we are very empathetic and can appreciate nuances that are often lost on the more hardy folk. We can astutely reveal you to yourself (whether or not you want this!). Alice Miller devotes a whole book to demonstrating how the gifted ones are the sensitive ones.[41] If you are sensitive, you probably tend to over-absorb the pain of others, which can make it difficult for you to flourish in your own life. People may be drawn to you for your perception and giftedness, but may unknowingly hang their baggage on the invisible 'hook' that your empathy offers. This entanglement, especially in family systems, can cause psychosomatic illnesses, displaced guilt and other neuroses. The sensitive person, therefore, will have to learn to hand back (with love – always with love) whatever does not belong to them.

Who is doing what to whom?

If you are the sensitive type, you will internalise other people's transference to the degree that you can end up feeling as if there is something wrong with you. Let's say there is somebody who is envious of you: if you are sensitive, you will pick it up atmospherically and then feel bad that you are making *them* feel bad! Phew! The result of this may be that you downplay yourself in an attempt to make them feel less envious. Now you are both entangled! Other people's thoughts and judgements can stick like Velcro. For example, when someone else is in bad mood, you might assume it has something to do with you; you feel you have done something wrong – again! Is it any wonder that you can feel like the world is just asking too much of you? Yes, it is – because you are allowing it. Ouch!

Do you find that when you declutter your house, you often find things belonging to others, things that need to be given back to their rightful owners? Well, likewise, with your psyche, you may discover that you are cluttered with dramas that, putting it bluntly, are none of your business! You might discover there are quite a few uninvited lodgers sitting in your solar plexus.

Perhaps we all need to do a bit of detoxing and a bit of housekeeping every now and then! Through the process of letting go, forgiving and handing back what does not belong, we honour the glorious temple of our being.

CHAPTER 10

All One Soul

A Unitive Vision

'You have your aunt's eyes,' I was told. My aunt, 'Sister B', as we called her, visited us once a year. Back in those days, nuns were not allowed to travel unaccompanied, so each summer she would arrive with another nun by her side. I presumed it was to lead her because she had no sight (needless to say, that was all *my* fault, because I had her eyes!). I didn't like that other nun and thought it would be better to send a guide dog instead! Sister B didn't read the newspapers or watch television – again, I presumed it was because I had taken her eyes. I would peer guiltily at her thick pink glasses, checking that there were definitely no eyes in there. She had a habit of peering into presses, fumbling around in private rooms and handbags; I reckoned it was pretty harmless since she couldn't see anything. She also had an annoying habit of folding her arms and striding up and down the floor making a clickety-click noise in her strange-looking shoes. Just as she reached one side of the room, she would look at the clock and then swish round again.

Unfortunately for me, in one of those swishes she did seem to momentarily regain her sight – she saw me right behind her! There I was, pacing clickety-click, my arms folded and a black cloth covering my head. Sister B's eyes were now fully visible and they were glaring right at me!

Connection: spanning across time and eternity

You may have been told that you have your aunt's eyes, your mother's brain, your father's temper etc. We pick up many genetic traits from previous generations. While our ancestors can release their gifts, such as a talent for music or art, to the present generation, they can also pass on what has been unfinished, the unacknowledged grief or unnamed secrets. What has not been resolved tends to get repeated; it gets passed on, usually in subtle but deeply impacting patterns. Perhaps it could be said that what one generation tries to bury, the next is forced to dig up. What was previously disowned or disembodied, the next generation is sometimes forced to own and to embody. 'Blessed are the gentle', we are told, because they 'shall have the earth as inheritance' (Mt 5: 4). Unfortunately, they inherit more than the earth – they sometimes inherit a whole host of uninvited guests claiming 'squatters' rights' in their psyche! This points to how intertwined we all are, and how we need to embrace both the blessing and the burden.

One field of energy

In his ground-breaking encyclical letter *Laudato Si'*, Pope Francis writes: 'Everything is related and we human beings are united as brothers and sisters on a wonderful pilgrimage, woven together by the love God has for each of his creatures and which also unites us in fond affection with brother sea, sister moon, brother river and mother earth.'[42] He writes that 'all of us are linked by unseen bonds and together form a kind of universal family, a sublime communion which fills us with a sacred, affectionate and humble respect.'[43]

We are spiritually, biologically and cognitively wired to be in connection with others. Relationships can offer us a pelvic push from the womb of self-isolation. Interestingly, the word 'person' in Greek means 'being in relationship'. The cosmos comprises a field of energies, structured in such a way that everything is interrelated. Researchers in quantum physics and science agree that the universe is an interconnected system; all things are part of each other, and all are related. Viktor Frankl discovered something similar: 'I wish to stress that the true meaning of life is to be discovered in the world rather than within man or his own psyche, as though it were a closed system.'[44] In Maslow's hierarchy of needs, 'belonging' is the third on the rung of priority of needs. The mystics also understood this; John of the Cross said, 'It seems to such a person that the entire universe is a sea of love in which it is engulfed, for conscious of the living point or centre of love within itself, it is unable to catch a sight of the boundaries of love.'[45]

Unitive glimpses

The unwashed saucepan on the hob had dribbles of leftover porridge. An old, retired shovel leaned against the overgrown ditch at the back of the garden. Nothing much was happening; a grey mist heralded another ordinary day after the glitter of Christmas. This drab January was something to be got through, a mere waiting room before the spring. Apart from the sound of a weary dog barking far away somewhere, a hoarse bird trying to sing and a church bell ringing in the distance, there was a silence so deep one could almost hear one's own heartbeat.

A light hail shower patterned itself on the window pane, and when it abated a weak, timid sun peered through the heavy clouds, sending little shafts of light through the window. For a few moments, it brightened and lit up the room, dancing momentarily off the porridge saucepan and the dusty mantelpiece, displaying a few bits of leftover Christmas tinsel. It lit up an ordinary room on an ordinary day; it lit up my heart, which also seemed to be covered with dust. For a few moments it was as if the veil was lifted, revealing a numinous way of seeing it all for the first time, where even the dust and the porridge dribbles looked sacred. It all looked like a beautiful mosaic, so much so that it awakened in me the desire to get out a paintbrush and capture it for all time. The sound of the barking dog, the hoarse bird, the church bell and my own breathing were as one. There was a wordless, formless quality about it all, a thinning of the boundary between the visible and invisible. Somehow Heaven and Earth seemed joined in a central axis and everything seemed to be as one. For some reason, I was acutely aware of those who had lived before me in this place, and were now beyond the veil but still connected. At the same time I felt comforted; love seemed to be behind it all, holding it all, imbuing it all. This comfort passed through my heart like an angel passing between two worlds. It was as if a door had opened into a realm where there was no separateness. For a brief moment I had withdrawn from the customary way of seeing a dull January afternoon, but soon, the moment vanished. Its shimmering quality began to fade. It was gone.

Later that evening, the sun looked jaundiced again; the porridge pot and the dusty furniture were once again mere reminders of the annoying chores to be done. However, the golden experience lived on somewhere, leaving a silent prayer of gratitude for old shovels, dusty mantelpieces, hail showers and porridge pots.

The Italian psychiatrist Roberto Assagioli says a unitive experience is 'characterised by a sense of joy and mental illumination that brings with it an insight into the meaning and purpose of life; it dispels many doubts, offers the solution of many problems, and gives an inner source of security. At the same time, there wells up a realisation that life is one, and an outpouring of love flows through the awakening individual toward his fellow beings and the whole of creation'.[45] The feeling that 'life is one' stayed with me long after that January experience and I was fascinated later to read how the Indian poet Rabindranath Tagore describes something similar: 'Suddenly in a minute, a veil seemed to be lifted from my eyes. I found the world rapt in an inexpressible glory with its waves of joy and beauty bursting and breaking on all sides. The thick cloud of sorrow that lay on my heart in many folds was pierced through and through by the light of the world, which was everywhere radiant. There was nothing and no one whom I did not love at that moment.'[47] Becoming aware of our interconnection is not always frothy and bubbly or filled with happy feelings; it can bring a deep pathos and poignancy, yet it reminds us we are not alone, especially on dull January afternoons.

Union or fusion?

She cuts the slice of toast and brings it to his mouth; she holds the knife and fork furtively and gazes at him attentively. They are now locked into a private little sanctum, inaccessible to anybody else. She butters another slice of toast and offers a piece to him as she leans across and rubs the back of his neck, leaving butter stains on his shirt. Huh, buttering him up, I muse. It is then I recognise her, and I text her to say hello. Her phone beeps, she looks at the number (not knowing I am two tables away). 'Anyone important?' her beloved asks. 'No one important,' I hear her say, as she switches off her phone and resumes gazing at him adoringly. 'Huh, how dare you– no one important,' I mutter. Eventually, leaving the food almost untouched, they leave hand in hand, giggling, locked into one another, with something much more compelling on their minds than eggs and bacon.

Some weeks later she is at the same table, this time on her own. My phone beeps, I read the text; 'Hi, great to see you, I'm across the way, will you join me?' Half-grudgingly, I go to her table. 'How is the romance going?' I ask. Her eyes deaden. 'All over,' she says, as she folds and unfolds the napkin. Her eyes begin to narrow as she mutters, 'And after all I did for him, he has the cheek to say he needed space ... the rat ... after I gave up everything, my friends ... everything ... *for him!*'

She was grieving the loss of her beloved, not realising that she had lost something even more vital – she had lost herself! Love is blind, we are sometimes told, especially when our saviour turns out to be a rodent! In this case love was blind enough to drive her to project all of her dependency needs totally onto one person. In looking to him for some magical potion that would deliver her from her feelings of separateness, she had created the very thing she was afraid of.

Relationship: crucible of growth

When we move towards interdependence (as against co-dependence), we cease trying to turn others into saviours who must rescue us from our aloneness. In truth, the ache of aloneness can never really fully be got rid of. Wise words come from Rainer Maria Rilke, who advised that 'a wonderful living side by side can grow up, if they succeed in loving the distance between them which makes it possible for each to see the other whole and against a wide sky'.[48] 'Loving the distance between us' is perhaps the most difficult and beautiful way for us all to live side by side.

Hollywood movies often portray the finding of happiness through finding 'the one'. It is often after many heartaches that we discover how everybody we enter into relationship with will partially delight us and partially disappoint us. This is not as depressing as it sounds, because people who know how to be alone but *choose* to be in relationship create strong foundations. There is an incompleteness and an insufficiency in all relationships and therein lies the beauty and mystery of our interconnection. Theologian Karl Rahner writes that 'in the torment of the insufficiency of everything attainable, we learn that ultimately in this world there is no finished symphony'.[49] It is into this unfinished symphony that Jesus gave his parting words to humanity when he prayed 'that they may all be one'. (Jn 17: 21)

CHAPTER 11

Buried Treasure

Gifts from the Unconscious

John travelled from one place to another, seldom satisfied, jobless, homeless, without friendship or community. He seemed to be one of those good guys who had had bad experiences repeatedly. He said that wherever he went, he felt that 'things just did not work out' for him. He said he longed for a life and a job that would give him a sense of purpose. All of us who knew him felt contradictory feelings of sympathy and irritation, knowing that he was a good man but that he seemed to mess up and sabotage everything for himself. Many prayed for a lucky break for him; people often tried to help, but in doing so seemed to get caught in the entanglement of his life. Eventually, a lucky break unfolded; a few friends found the 'perfect job' for him, one that seemed to fit perfectly with what he said he had been looking for. They approached a man who agreed to create a job for John in his own business, and an informal interview was set up. Excitedly, they told John about this newfound opportunity, about which he seemed delighted (although they also sensed a reticence in him). They enthusiastically outlined all the possibilities now available to him: a new beginning, a new identity, a proper home, the possibility of an interesting career and so forth. Some of us even helped to organise for his stuff to be packed, bought some furniture for him and helped him fill out forms for the interview. He agreed, at least on the surface, that this lucky break was wonderful. Weeks passed, and we eventually contacted him to check how he was getting on in the new job. He fell silent and after a long pause he admitted that he had turned it down; in fact, he hadn't even gone to the interview. He tried to drum up some excuse, but he knew, and everyone else knew, that he had sabotaged it – the same way he had sabotaged every other good thing in his life. He had now landed himself back in the very same position: directionless, jobless, purposeless.

Destroyer of the good

What unconscious force pushed John to destroy what was good? Why did he push away something that he had so desperately wanted? The answer lay in his story; John had felt worthless as a child, and was made to feel that he would 'never succeed at anything'. He believed he was a failure and so, as an adult, he set up situations that would endorse that belief. Consequently, and unknowingly, he continued to reject whatever might dispute his feelings of worthlessness. Whenever a door of opportunity opened he slammed it shut again. Perhaps it was just too much, and it didn't fit his old narrative. Sadly, his deep feelings of non-deserving were not addressed and they were therefore running and ruining his life. Those of us who tried to help him may even have added to the problem; by enabling and making excuses for him, we were preventing his facing up to his pattern and choices. We were rendering him powerless by doing things that he needed to do for himself. We were actually pushing against another force inside him, some unconscious coding that insisted he was worthless. For as long as he refused to look at his own beliefs about himself, any outer 'help' would not make a difference. Eventually we had to withdraw, so that he would see the tragedy of his own self-sabotage and the underlying reasons why he was not allowing himself to 'succeed at anything'.

Recognising sabotage

Self-sabotage is a process whereby we put obstacles in our own way. It is a subtle and unconscious dynamic that allows us to put happiness out of reach for ourselves. When we are entangled in self-sabotage, we postpone and prevent the changes we need to make. While we might seem to be going in the direction of something positive, there may be another force pulling us back. Somebody once described this as being equivalent to driving a car while the handbrake is still on. If we don't know it's on, the car will stick between two opposing forces. When we are caught between two internal forces, a pull and a counter-pull, there is often an old, unconscious belief telling us that we are undeserving. We might even attract situations and circumstances that will sabotage anything new, so we stay within our familiar and prescribed range of possibilities. Unconscious forces can hold us back from living our lives fully or from achieving our goals and dreams. While we might be in a place of misery, we often choose to stay there because at least we know what to expect: more misery!

How to be miserable – in a few easy steps

Bookshelves are lined with 'how to be happy' books. Maybe knowing what makes us miserable is equally important. It is important that we know how much we drain ourselves (and everyone around us) when we believe in negative outcomes, engage in comparisons, self-pity, unconscious victim stances etc.

I remember once meeting a woman who held deep unconscious beliefs centred around being undeserving. She struggled financially and constantly lamented, 'Sure, nothing good ever happens to me.' She inherited a substantial sum of money, but within a very short time she had lost most of it through taking unwise risks. The universe handed her a gift and she handed it right back. She sabotaged herself and so was back in the same limiting situation, while – once again – repeating, 'Sure, nothing good ever happens to me.'

Envy is another way of sabotaging our own growth. George Bernard Shaw tells us that we must channel our good fortune towards something creative, instead of following destructive forces, 'being a force of nature instead of a clod of ailments and grievances complaining that the world will not devote itself to making you happy'.[50]

The 'force of nature' is very visible on this early spring morning; nature is waking up, the tree outside my window sways proudly in her new cloak of green. Our spirit-filled universe sings a song of beauty with its lush green fields, trees and budding plants. The colour green speaks to us of newness and growth; interestingly, green is also considered to be the colour of envy! Could there be possibilities for growth in our envy? Could our little green-eyed demons actually steer us away from our 'clod of ailments and grievances' towards recognising the abundance of what we already have? Instead of looking over our shoulders and making ourselves miserable, could we channel the greenness of our envy to begin to grow our own dreams?

'Anyone could do that,' Patricia insisted when a friend of hers produced her first music album. 'Are you jealous?' I asked. 'Not at all,' she replied quickly. 'Sure, if I tried I could do it just as good, probably better.' 'Why not try, then?' I asked. She shrugged her shoulders, 'Ah, couldn't be bothered, albums aren't bought much nowadays.' After a long silence, her unconscious fears emerged and she said nervously and in a less forceful voice, 'Yeah, I suppose I am a teeny bit jealous. I would love to have done what she did, I am just too afraid and so I regret that I never used my singing voice.' Once she had unmasked the little green-eyed demon and saw the fear lurking beneath it, she stopped acting it out and decided instead to act on it. No longer victim to her jealousy, she eventually went for singing lessons; she allowed her envy to be a motivator. When 'acted *out*', her jealousy actually immobilised her, but when 'acted *on*' it had the energy to redirect her towards what she really wanted.

When we are truthful with ourselves about our grievances, they can be transmuted into something else: into a more altruistic giving and receiving of life's gifts. Our reactions carry a map for us to read carefully. While it is tempting to take those go-getters down a peg or two by muttering disparaging comments about them, perhaps instead we could allow them to inspire us. While it is understandable that we would gripe about why someone else seems to have an easy ride up the mountain while we have to puff and pant step by step, it might help to remember that when we compare, we despair!

Shifting perspective

We were standing in line at the card shop. The woman in front started a conversation, pointing out the funny anniversary card that she was purchasing for her husband. 'It's ten years next week,' she said wistfully. 'Same as myself,' I replied. She went on to recall the wedding day, saying, 'I got this beautiful bouquet of flowers and I left them in the house on the morning of the wedding and hadn't time to run back for them.' In an almost sulking tone, she said 'I hate, even now, seeing the photos of myself walking up the aisle without my lovely bouquet.' She turned her attention to me, asking, 'And how was your day?' I replied, 'Likewise, I don't like looking at photos of myself walking up the aisle ... without my lovely mother!' I explained how my mother had an accident a week before the wedding. Horrified, she asked, 'And, how is she now?' 'She died soon after,' I replied. A bit embarrassed, she changed the subject. Perhaps her memory of walking up the aisle without her 'lovely flowers' faded into oblivion when she considered what it would have been like to walk up without her 'lovely mother'.

The glass half empty mentality, 'catastrophic thinking', causes us to lose perspective, as we look for the dark cloud in front of every silver lining! Sometimes, when we look beyond our own disappointments, we gain a necessary perspective. This allows us to see our own dilemma with new eyes; we can begin to find acceptance in an imperfect world, a world where loss and suffering are an intrinsic part.

Digging for truth

Self-awareness can give us the key to opening our own internal caves where treasures are buried. They are often the caves we are most afraid to enter. Sometimes, the material in our dreams gives us subtle indications as to what is in our subconscious. What you dream at night may be reflecting back an underlying issue that you cannot yet access with your conscious mind. Whether the issue is around sabotage, envy or catastrophic thinking, it never helps to say, 'It is my fault because I am doing this to myself', nor does it help if someone else says 'you are doing this to yourself'. We will, in such cases, only retreat further into our self-sabotage. We need instead to gently coax out the underlying beliefs that have kept such scripts in place. Through self-awareness, we begin to dig out the old repeating habits that unconsciously hold us back.

Taking charge of our mental health

A habit is formed when we unconsciously follow old neurological trails that are created through neurons firing off one another. These neurons are the very small brain cells that make up the nervous system. Each time we follow a particular trail, it becomes more embedded and therefore gets stronger.

For example, if you repeatedly sabotage good things or postpone important decisions, one part of your brain will keep returning to this habit like an old repeating record. The stress response then increases the production of inflammatory chemicals in our body.

Once we can identify the old belief systems that have been keeping this sabotage in place, we are then able to take charge of our brain in introducing new healthier neural trails. Our brain clings to what we know (the law of repetition). By introducing a new habitual thought pattern and repeating it over and over again, the brain will then 'normalise' it and a new record is set in place. However, especially at the beginning, there is a danger that the old gravitational pull will create a scenario that results in you giving up too soon before the new thought pattern has taken root and before it has become normalised. The more we persevere, the more resilient and resourceful we will feel about ourselves, the more we will have mastery over our mental health and the more we will produce the motivating chemicals (neurotransmitters) dopamine and serotonin.

In mythological stories, the protagonist picks up his sword and charges forth, right into the mouth of the dragon. He eventually triumphs over what has been threatening or chasing him. Likewise, on our own heroic journey to wholeness we sometimes have to face, head on, what has been automating our lives through unconscious sabotage, envy etc. So, to triumph over the negative, ask yourself, 'What do I need to do, believe in, or allow for myself?' Perhaps the most important word in this question is the word 'allow'. Perhaps I can even take a step towards *allowing* something new to happen today.

CHAPTER 12

The Bottom Line

The Beauty of Imperfection

'You can't wear a bikini at forty-seven,' she said glumly, flicking through a holiday brochure while waiting in a queue at the travel agents. 'Yes,' she continued, now directing the conversation to me, 'I heard it on the radio.' Personally, I thought it had been quite a while since she saw forty-seven, but nevertheless I asked, 'Why do you let others decide the "bottom line"?' (pardon the pun). 'Oh,' she said, 'if I went out in a bikini at my age people would say I had an awful cheek!' ('Awful cheek,' I giggled to myself; I didn't know if she heard exactly what she said there.)

We interject things like 'nobody at my age', or beliefs such as 'It's not okay to be seen ... ', and we then 'squeeze' ourselves into other people's measurements of what is, or is not, socially acceptable. We wear ideas and worlds that are just too small for us. In trying to fit in, we often end up resenting those who impose such standards and, worse still, we end up hating ourselves for complying. It is too easy to become enslaved to the numerous social trends that create yardsticks for how we are to look and behave in society. This conformity can deaden our own unique way of being in the world, evicting joy from our hearts and leaching the creativity from our souls. Over-conformity tends to morph us into fabricated images of who we think we *should* be. We thus become victims of an advertising world where the motivation of profitability is selling us an artificial version of happiness. We might, for example, find ourselves buying clothes we cannot afford, with money we don't have, to look like celebrities we probably don't even like! If the purpose of your life narrows down to this, you begin to betray the creative force that sent you into this world. This betrayal causes a gnawing and relentless pain in the soul.

The bottom line: who decides?

The dieting industry seems to be something akin to a new religion: bookshops are glutted with diet manuals promoting the attainment of perfect bodies. While we certainly need to aim for fitness and health, we can do so without striving for the goal of a perfect body (which becomes yet another empty crock at the end of the rainbow). Some self-help and 'spiritual' programmes even suggest that a weakness in the body is somehow indicative of being out of alignment with the divine forces. At best, this is superficial; at worst, it makes judgements about those who are ill. Furthermore, it completely and erroneously discounts that there are those who live life to the full, often heroically, within limitations in health and in body. I am thinking here of Joanne O'Riordan, intelligent, humorous, ambitious, who, while only about 20 inches tall, has nevertheless touched people enormously. She has a condition called 'Total Amelia' (born without limbs), but has faced every challenge and barrier with which she has been presented, and refuses to see herself as a victim. On her sixteenth birthday she addressed the United Nations Conference, refusing to entertain the word 'impossible', but rephrasing it 'I'm possible'.

Real heroes can live vibrantly within their limitations and stand bravely in their humanity. In their overcoming of obstacles, they revolutionise how human imperfection can be perceived. They teach us not to become over-identified with our physical form, and teach us to never forget the formless, eternal dimension of who we really are.

Scripture advises us 'not to worry about your life and what you are to eat, nor about your body and how you are to clothe it' (Mt 6: 25). It assures us that, while we need all of those things, we are 'more than' our bodies. Society, on the other hand, tells us to fight any sign of ageing, or any impending bodily decay, and to seek permanence in an impermanent world.

Blessed wrinkles

I was stopped by a woman at the cosmetic counter as I rushed through the department store. 'Excuse me,' she said as she stepped out in front of me with a large cosmetic smile. 'What moisturiser do you use'? 'Oh', I said, 'a bit of this and a bit of that.' Unimpressed, she proceeded, 'Would you like to try some of our latest ... ?' 'Ah no,' I answered, 'I don't need anything.' 'But what do you do about these?' she asked, pointing her manicured fingers towards the tapestry of fine wrinkles around my eyes! She really went for the jugular, presuming she was on to a winner here – a woman in her fifties with a few wrinkles! Unfortunately for her, she found the wrong woman, because in my hierarchy of concerns, that little mosaic of life's relics around my eyes does not feature very high in the pecking order. Eventually, her wrinkle-free eyes narrowed, and her smile moved on to the next imperfect passer-by!

Hankering after youth means missing the miracle of who we are now; it is like discounting the beauty of autumn by hankering after summer. The greatest impediment to contentment is created by railing against life as it is, and trying to force it to be what it isn't.

In the dark of the night, our existential fears can well up from beneath even the most perfect skincare regime. The fears we might try to allay by pushing ourselves in excessive gym routines or obsessive diets can then return to haunt us. It becomes exhausting when we are trying desperately to hide our ageing or imperfect bodies; it is like trying to stabilise your feet on a foundation that keeps slipping and sliding. Perhaps awareness of our infallibility and incompleteness keeps us from moving too far away from our humanity or from becoming inflated with our own grandiosity. I remember an elderly priest who, with severe Parkinson's disease, could not coordinate the movements of his own body, and could not get any words out of his mouth. However, he communicated something that has stayed with me indelibly; it shone from his eyes. I learned more from those eyes than I did from any philosopher or theologian. There is a wound in all of us, and perhaps that very weakness creates the entry for the light, or for what we call 'grace'. Society has made a pathology of human vulnerability, deeming it something to be cured or fixed. Nowhere in scripture are we promised that an encounter with the divine will bring an insurance against vulnerability or imperfection. Jacob found himself wounded and walking with a limp following his encounter with an angel. As a young girl Helen Keller lost her sight, yet she is known for her extraordinary depth of spirit. Beethoven continued to write wonderful music after he became deaf. Maria, an elderly sister now carrying a recurrent malaria infection, speaks with poignancy and gratitude for the children she worked with in Africa. While there is weakness in her body, there is joy in her stride; she has not allowed herself to be a victim of any biological fate. People with very agile and strong bodies can have hearts that are closed and devoid of warmth or passion. In contrast, there are heroes who carry a weakness in the body, but fire in the spirit. Christopher Reeve, the film actor who brought the fictional comic book character Superman to life on the big screen, had to become a hero for himself after his tragic horse-riding accident in 1995.

I have often railed against God about various limitations in my own health and strength (most of them inherited). I expected there would be one big grand miracle and, hey presto, I would finally become 'superwoman'! The only presto moments, however, were a steady and continuous assurance that something greater than my imperfect self would sustain me, a call to trust that grace would be sufficient (2 Co 12: 9). Some day I still hope to be 'superwoman', but in the meantime, I'm content to plod along with the imperfect St Paul, who also was told to rely on grace regarding his 'thorn in the flesh' (2 Co 12: 7). It can, of course, be frustrating when the fire is stronger than the physical frame, when we might, understandably, wish that God would put his fire somewhere else! However, any fighting of our human condition creates resistance, and this in turn depletes our resources even further.

Perfect bodies, imperfectlives
We cannot summon perfection or wholeness at gunpoint; we cannot abort every weakness in pursuit of perfect

bodies, perfect lives. The pursuit of some idealised image of perfection can become our cocaine! We wear ourselves out by holding in contempt a body that refuses to move fast enough, and by longing to be like those who seem to have limitless energy. However, those who ruthlessly and constantly push beyond their own humanity tend to carry an underground irritation and intolerance for those who are not moving as fast as they are. They try to be like little gods, unable to delegate and depend on others. In the hero's journey and in many other myths, the meeting of an elder or wise figure can be a turning point – they illuminate a blind spot and often teach us something about humility.

In the Old Testament, Moses held a responsible position wherein his wisdom was sought by many (perhaps he could not delegate). Jethro, his father-in-law, who was an elder, a wise man, challenged him: 'Why do you do this for the people, why sit here alone with the people standing round you from morning till evening?' (Ex 18: 14)

In my work with people in counselling and spiritual guidance one of the key themes that keeps returning is this inability to delegate; it frequently causes symptoms of burnout. Sometimes, when I have attempted to challenge this, I have been met with responses like, 'But you don't understand how important my role is; it all depends on me. If I don't do it, nobody else will.' Is this familiar? Sometimes I have to be a Jethro figure. We are 'limited' through age, circumstances and health, but, as singer and songwriter Leonard Cohen reminds us: 'There is a crack in everything, That's how the light gets in.' It usually takes us all a long time to learn this lesson.

'I'm off on holidays. I'm looking forward to just chilling out,' I said to a colleague. 'Huh, *you*, chilling out?' She laughed aloud. Then she straightened up and looked at me with great seriousness, 'Cop on, you *know* you will take work with you, you *always* do.' Indignant, I wanted to shoot back at this Jethro, 'How dare you!' A week later, while I was sitting out in the sun after breakfast armed with papers and journals, the waiter asked me (in his broken English), 'You here on work, or you holiday?' 'Holiday,' I cheerily answered. He looked at my stack of papers, rolled his eyes to heaven and walked away. 'Another bloody Jethro, why don't they f**k off,' I muttered as I resolutely resumed my work. Weeks later, in the doctor's surgery, 'Just a bit run down,' I explained. 'What do you do to chill out?' she asked. I sat up, and excitedly started to describe how I had just sanded down and painted all the chairs and the kitchen cupboards. She looked at my fingers, still coated with paint, raised an eyebrow, while muttering under her breath, 'I asked what you do to *chill out*!' I finally got it – this Jethro got through!

Trying to be everything to everyone means we get so diluted that eventually there is nobody 'there' when people encounter us. When we are 'full on' all of the time, we lose our depth. We need deliberately to create restorative time to address this.

Finite and fabulous

We live in a world of duality: light and dark, youth and ageing, winters of loss and joys of summer. We do not have to bypass the human condition in quest of some supernatural state. St Augustine once reminded us, 'Make humanity your journey and you will arrive at God.' The saints and enlightened ones lived lives oriented with fire and purpose, but never denied their weakness and vulnerability. John of the Cross writes from a place of his own vulnerability:

> *My love, where are you hidden?*
> *Why have you left me sorrowing alone?*
> *I followed you unbidden,*
> *But like a stag you'd flown*
> *Wounded, I called, but you, my love, were gone.*[51]

'Wounded I call you' is often our prayer too when it comes from an honest place within us. The light of authenticity is more magnetic and attractive than any perfect body or wrinkle-free face. 'When the world meets people whose centre of gravity is within their authentic selves, it draws close to them like moths to a magnet.'[52] We are fallible and fabulous, beautifully perfect in our imperfection. Maybe we have less need to hanker after 'having it all' when we know that we are finite beings resourced and animated by an Infinite God. When we know that our lives interface with the paschal mystery, we discover that it is when we are weak that we are strong. Maybe, therefore, it will be through our open (and wounded) hearts, and through our wrinkled hands (manicured by living and loving), that we will, one day, be connected in eternity.

Befriending impermanence

Scripture tells us that knowing the shortness of our life brings wisdom: 'Teach us to count how few days we have, and so gain wisdom of heart' (Ps 90: 12). We tend to airbrush out all conversations about death and dying, but this only results in us denying our fears. We like to imagine that we can face the final curtain filled with emotional stoicism and swagger down the corridor to eternity! However, denying our fear of death is one way to be totally defined by it.

Joseph Campbell tells us that befriending our death is a key stage in the hero's journey. 'The last act in the biography of the hero is that of the death or departure. Here the whole sense of the life is epitomised. Needless to say, the hero would be no hero if death held for him any terror: the first condition is reconciliation with the grave.'[53] Facing our fear of death can set us free; it reminds us that everything and everyone in our life is an impermanent gift. Trying to make permanent what is transient only creates resistance. Life keeps changing, the body keeps ageing, but if we keep digging our heels in, we stop the flow. Perhaps all of our death fears are really a fear of letting go of the ego. We can put huge energy into defending, propping up and protecting our ego. We can become so identified with it that any slight against our role or our achievements can feel like a threat to our very being; in fact, it can sometimes feel as if we are physically dying. The poor ego will desperately try to engineer a few more strategies in trying to hang on, which in turn creates tension and struggle. Perhaps we will discover that we have less need to dig our heels into our illusive permanence if we know that at the end, just as we are born out of love, we will return to love.

The alchemical fire

I stood in the driveway looking at the flames rising up into the sky. It was wild and fierce as it mercilessly shredded my life's belongings. The fire brigade had the light still flashing as the men worked to quench the fire, which by now had ripped through the building. Eventually, only the smell of smouldering timber remained, filling the night air. A semblance of my belongings lay in ashes before me. I walked a few yards away from the scene, I turned around and looked back, thinking *What is left of my life? Who am I now?* When the numbness wore off a little, I felt a strange feeling of both terror and grace (mostly terror). Most of what I had cherished was gone, yet it felt like a grace just to be alive, to know that my heart was still beating and that my feet were on the ground. Strangely, even in the shock I was aware of something more, as if I was being held by forces and entities beyond my grasp; I stretched out my arms to the sky – for whom I did not know. I looked up into the silent depths, full of wordless questions. Somehow, with the roof of my life burned down, the stars above seemed very near; there was an unspeakable knowing that I was not alone. I was not fully in my body, but not entirely out of it either. The alchemical fire had burned up all that had held me safe in the world! While I eventually built up my 'normal' life again, I never quite forgot that night, and what, as Tagore said, 'had entered the room of my heart through the ruins'.

That night when the storm broke down my doors,
I did not know that you entered my room through the ruins.
For the lamp was blown out, and it became dark;
I stretched my arms to the sky
for whom I did not know
I waited in the darkness as if in a dream.
That the storm was your banner,
I did not know.
When the morning came
I saw you there
Pervading all the emptiness of my abode.

Fire can be both terrifying and transformative, burning away the transient from the eternal. The Hebrew people heard the voice of the living God speaking from the heart of the fire (Dt 4: 34). The Irish people saw the fire lit by St Patrick on the hill of Tara. The memory of the fire on that starry night never left my consciousness; the terrifying crackling of the flames, yet alongside it the memory of the exquisite beauty of a starlit sky. The whole experience instilled in me an awareness of life's fragility and a greater urgency to live it more fully. I didn't expect a loss like this could be a freeing experience; I suppose I was *surprised by fire!*

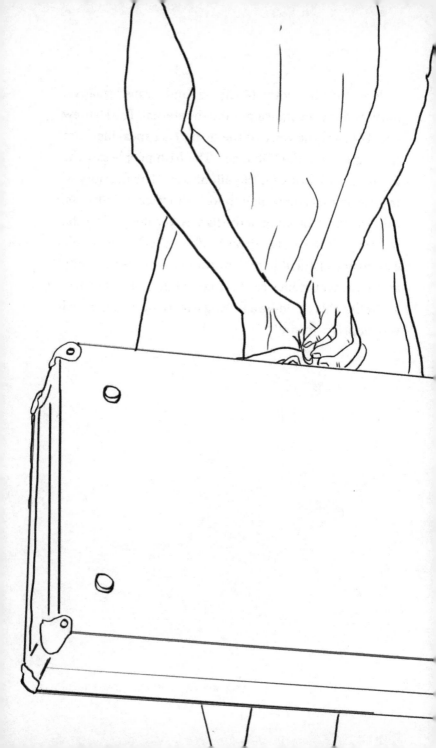

PART FOUR

Homecoming

Chapter 13

Compassion

The Greatest Treasure

It was a Friday evening in November, and we were sitting in a café in Central Dublin, when news broke about the terrorist attacks in Paris. Many lives were lost, numerous people were injured; it was now a city seized with terror. As we watched images of Paris on the television screen, the shift in atmosphere was palpable. A nervousness seemed to envelop everyone; it drew a café of strangers into an interconnected unity. A collective resonance swirled in the room; there was a perceptible sense of togetherness, not just with one another but with those in Paris and with humankind all over the world. However, after the initial shock of first hearing the news, people began gradually to regroup and regain their separateness, each getting back into survival mode. Snippets of conversations began, some even argumentative. One person said, 'They should retaliate now'; another said, 'Thank God, it's not us.' The kaleidoscope was shifting to more self-protective knee-jerk reactions. The comment that grated on me was this one: 'Thank God it's Paris, and not us.' Had we forgotten so quickly again that we are all one soul?

Quivering of the heart

In Buddhist teachings compassion is sometimes described as 'the quivering of the heart' in response to suffering. No doubt all our hearts quivered that day but we tried, each in our own way, to protect ourselves from involvement in the pain. Our reactive responses are often heavily biased: we differentiate between our 'in group' and those outside our field of identification. Genuine compassion must include those we consider to be different, even those who threaten our cosy circles of belonging.

Albert Einstein tells us 'a human being is part of the whole, called by us a "Universe". He experiences himself, his thoughts and feelings, as something separate from the rest – a kind of optical delusion of consciousness. Our task must be to free ourselves from this prison by widening our circle of compassion to embrace all living creatures.'[54]

To 'widen our circle of compassion' is very challenging – usually at the first mention of suffering we feel so powerless that it is easier to contract against feeling the pain. For example, we might see a homeless person and start ranting about why he doesn't go and get a job. What we are really doing is trying to catapult ourselves out of this powerless feeling (or maybe the guilty feeling that we are passing him by).

We might do it when we hear of starving children, or of those caught in a natural disaster. Often, when it is too painful to feel, we reflexively complain about governments, and how it is their fault, and how there is no point in trying to do anything because the money doesn't go where it is most needed etc. While there may be some truth in all of this, turning away is, nevertheless, an act of disconnection; it severs us from our seat of compassion. Our post-modern culture has elevated self-care, self-development and self-sufficiency as the ultimate goals. It is not easy to get the balance whereby you neither distance yourself from other people's suffering, nor become so consumed by it that you get drained. I know of an elderly woman who takes the newspaper into the chapel when saying her morning prayers, 'so that I know what, and who to pray for', she says. In her prayer, she sends compassion to places and people she has never met. She truly connects with the place where 'her heart quivers'.

Softening the armour

With wild eyes and unkempt red hair, she muttered to herself, oblivious of anyone else in her path, and indifferent to any traffic on the street. Whenever she raised her wine bottle, the oncoming cars and buses would screech to a halt. She would then cross the road regardless of whether the lights were red or green. Head and wine bottle held high, she would wave angrily at the traffic if they so much as dared to rev the engine or resume driving too soon. Sometimes, she would stop in the middle of the road and take a long leisurely swig from the bottle, while drivers waited nervously. 'Don't mind them losers,' she would mutter aloud, while offering them the two fingers. On other occasions, she would be seen in churches giving an ultimatum to the statues, directing the wine bottle accusingly at them (and occasionally giving a few of the statues the two fingers also!). She would then 'reverently' make the sign of the cross and stride out angrily. All the while, she would keep shouting, 'They're not going to get you' (I couldn't quite make out if she was saying this to herself, or to the bottle of wine). 'She's off her head,' people said as they tried to avoid her, probably secretly terrified in case they got a swipe of her tongue – or the bottle.

I haven't seen her for many years. I presume she has since died. People said that she had nobody belonging to her in this world; she had lost her family early in life. On hearing that, I began to understand why she needed constantly to reassure herself that 'nobody's going to get you'. Perhaps if she had met somebody with whom she felt safe enough to tell her story her life might have turned out differently. Perhaps she might have found some compassion for herself and for her loss, and so would not have needed to act it out with wine bottles and statues.

Compassion is the hallmark of those who have come home to their own centre. It is the ultimate gift of the transformed life. It is compassion alone that can soften the hard armouring around the heart. Some people fear that compassion is a kind of self-indulgent sentimental practice, or they fear that it will leave them too open and 'soft' in a harsh world. Psychologist Carl Rodgers considered 'unconditional positive regard' to be the most important ingredient in any process of healing. It allows us safely to tell our story to others and, perhaps more importantly, it allows us to tell our stories to ourselves! Usually, the broken places in us do not so much need fixing, as to be met with compassion. In the gospel of St Luke, the well-known story of the Prodigal Son parallels the hero's journey. The son leaves home, travels to a distant land and eventually discovers his real hunger, and so he begins to make the journey home. It is a story of compassion; while the son left his father geographically, he remained inside his father's compassionate heart. 'While he was still a long way off, his father saw him and was moved with pity. He ran to the boy, clasped him in his arms and kissed him' (Lk 15: 20).

Self-compassion

Perhaps what we find most difficult is the extension of compassion towards ourselves. Most people in psychological pain have high levels of shame and self-criticism. Self-compassion is increasingly recognised by psychologists, therapists and neuroscientists as a prerequisite to healing many conditions of anxiety and depression. What has more recently been referred to as the 'science of compassion' describes not just an emotion, but something that acts as a motivator, a catalyst and a therapeutic tool. When we visit our wounds with compassion, we discover, paradoxically, that the medicine is often *in* the wound. As Jung says, 'I myself stand in need of the arms of my own kindness; I am the enemy to be loved.'[55] You cannot fake compassion; the 'fake it till you make it' strategy might work in matters related to building confidence or success, but rarely for the deeper things of the heart.

Mercy, not sacrifice

I went to America to work as a volunteer on a project dealing with children from troubled homes in New York's inner city. I had given up my job for a few months to be part of the project to 'help' these troubled children. One day we were sitting on the grass and I was giving a talk to them (on the theme of compassion). I noticed Jason, a nine-year-old boy, was not reading the notes I had given to them, but was staring at me intensely. A bit unnerved, I eventually asked him if he needed something. He said in a slow and serious tone, 'You don't like us, do you?' I began to protest profusely, but he continued, 'No, I don't think you really, really like us.' He went on to clarify, 'You don't like us in the way Sister Liz likes us'. (Sister Liz was a wild, laughing nun who chewed gum, listened to country music and whistled as she drove her jeep, which was usually full of kids.) My stomach clenched and I felt weak inside. I waited for an apology, but it didn't come. This was a real facedown moment for me, especially since all the other kids were watching to see my reaction. I tried my best to continue the class and to keep a safe distance from their dangerously perceptive radar. I went back to my room muttering, 'After all I did, coming all the way out here to help them, here I am unwaged, sweltering hot, sleeping in horrible bunk beds, how dare he ... '. Suddenly, a line from scripture ran through my mind: 'Go and learn the meaning of the words; what I want is mercy not sacrifice' (Mt 9: 13). The internal arguments subsided a little as I gradually surrendered to the possibility that there might actually be some invitation in this difficult encounter. I sat in silence, reflecting on what the child had said to me, and wondered why he had interpreted a lack of compassion in me. Through much reflection, not just that evening, but each of the subsequent evenings, I found myself slowly encountering another child – the one inside my own heart; a child from whom I was also keeping a safe distance, and who was also in need of my compassion.

A compassionate self-acceptance is a prerequisite to being able to extend compassion to others: 'The acceptance of oneself is the essence of the moral problem and the epitome of a whole outlook on life.'[56] I am still very grateful that I encountered this little New York straight-shooter!

To suffer with

Compassion is not something that is extended from the healthy towards the sick, the strong towards the weak, or between the lost and the found. It is a relationship where we stand together in our shared humanity, where we are both healers and wounded for one another. The word compassion comes from the Latin word *compati*, meaning 'to suffer with'. At the root of compassion is the belief that you and I are not separate but, in fact, *You are Me, and I am You*. Author and psychiatrist Gerald G. May tells us that 'we are so intimately joined in Divine mystery, that when a single one of us falls we are all wounded, and when a single one breathes freely and opens to the exquisitely painful ecstasy of love we are all nourished'.[57]

Compassion: the silent language

My mother's cousin Fr Jerome called at around three o'clock every Sunday. He was a man of few words and yet, despite his poor eyesight, he drove over twenty miles each week to visit my mother, and they sat mainly in silence. He barely ate anything, as his stomach was always 'giving him trouble' following the numerous surgeries he had had to undergo since returning home from the missions. Each Sunday, the noisy engine of his car could be heard revving back and forth as he tried to park by ramming the vehicle up against the side of the kerb. Eventually, the engine would be turned off, the car would be left halfway up on the footpath (with the rear end sticking out into the road), and the lights usually left switched on. 'He is here,' my mother would say, opening the door wide and leading him into the front room. There would be a tray ready – a pot of tea, two cups and a few biscuits, the soft ones that she knew he could digest. An occasional few syllables could be heard, alongside the crackling of the fire and the ticking of the clock. Both were fragile, quiet, frequently ill, and shared everything by sharing nothing. Something special passed between them in those silences. They would both doze off, and whoever would wake up first might say a few words and then another cup of tea would be poured. Eventually, he would look at his watch. 'Are you heading off? Be careful now on the road, it will be dark soon,' she would say as he left the room. She would sit for a long while after he had left, rosary beads in her hand, lips barely moving, praying he would get back safely before dark. The car would zigzag down the hill, swerving out of the way of the unfortunate oncoming drivers. The whole ritual would be repeated at three o'clock the following Sunday, and every Sunday until that awful day when we had to ring him to tell him about the accident. It was a week before my wedding; my mother was supposed to give me away and he was to preside. They had both been so excited, and she was arranging who would collect him so he wouldn't be driving in the dark. At three o'clock, nearly halfway through the wedding ceremony, he zigzagged up the aisle, looking lost, directionless, as if he was looking for her, even while knowing she wouldn't be there. 'Hard times,' he said to me later when he explained how he couldn't join us for the wedding reception, as he would need to 'be home before the dark'. After my mother's death, he surrendered his driving licence, and the three o'clock sound of the engine revving outside the door was never heard again.

I did not meet him again until I visited him before his own death, where, in the throes of advanced Alzheimer's, he managed to whisper, 'How is she?' I didn't remind him that she had died. It wasn't long afterwards that he joined her. Maybe he heard her whisper, 'He is here', as the door opened to where they could rest in silence and never again have *to leave before the dark*.

A compassionate understanding united them in their silences. Below the surface of conversation, they shared a presence that lived on in the heart, even when the faculties of the mind had left.

Many quiet heroes transform our world, not only through words but also through the gaps between the words, the pauses between the notes in the music, the compassion in what they say and what they do not say.

CHAPTER 14

Ham, Music and Kisses

A Living Spirituality

There was something about Saturday nights: *Céilí House* on the radio, shoes all shiny and polished, ready for the morning, and the aroma of ham on the boil. We would frequently be chided for lifting the cover of the saucepan and stealing chunks of ham (to test it, we argued). The music, the shiny shoes and the ham were like glimpses of heaven – until we would hear that familiar but dreaded 'Come on, everyone, time for the Rosary'. The music was switched off, chairs screeched along the floor, we got on our knees, leaned into the chairs, and straight away we were off … like greyhounds after a hare! A marathon of Hail Marys tripped off our tongues. Even the hand in the old grandfather clock seemed to gallop along with us. Eventually, as we neared the end (hoping the others had lost count), I would shoot in a Glory Be after just six Hail Marys. (I might chance just *five* Hail Marys if *Dallas* was on that particular night!) I would stare with anticipation at the heavy cloth covering the television set, kept securely in place by the rabbit ears aerial. Maybe tonight we would finally find out who shot JR. Ah, at last, the final Amen, signalling the time for beads to be hung up on the side of the dresser until tomorrow night. Up we would sprint – time for *Dallas*, cloth rolled up, television switched on. Now, the drama is getting interesting: shoulder-padded Sue Ellen is fighting once again with the cunning JR. Pretty Pam is crying again and being consoled by dishy Bobby. Suddenly and abruptly the television is switched off, and quickly covered by the heavy cloth as the rabbit ears are firmly and without negotiation slammed on top. And all because Bobby kissed Pam! The message is clear: in this Valley of Tears and Rosaries, there must be no ham, no music and definitely no kissing!

Memories like these live on in the psyche of many Irish people. For some, their childhood devotional practices, such as the Rosary, were warm, meditative and deeply foundational. For others, they felt like a constant appeasing of some distant object of veneration, which was more focused on making reparation to a punitive God than on receiving compassion from a divine maternal love.

Much of our early upbringing involved an implicit splitting of spirit and body, an elevation of all things spiritual and a contempt for the world, the earthier things. This disembodied piety led to dangerous repression, creating neurotic splits in the psyche; a kind of monophysite heresy (where Christ is seen as divine but not human). ' 'Twas grace that taught my heart to fear and grace my fears relieved', the old hymn goes; yes, it surely was an 'amazing grace' how some religious practices, while being oppressive, may have also set a seed. While much of our upbringing may have 'taught the heart to fear', it also created an impetus to search, to go beyond the hellfire, and discover the heart fire. An incarnational faith can illuminate how a prayer as beautiful as the Rosary can help us to meditate on our human walk with the human Christ; it invites us to be fully here for all of it – including the ham and the kisses.

Living faith

True spirituality is a recognition that we are all inextricably connected to one another by a power greater than all of us, and that our connection to that power ignites what is deepest and most noble in the human heart. True Christianity does not end at a devotional practice, statue or shrine, but moves into and permeates every area of our lives in a life-giving and transformative way. True spirituality is a living relationship, not a set of concepts and ideologies. When asked about his message, Jesus says, 'Come and see'; in other words, spend time with him. Surrender to a higher power; while it feels like defeat and death to the poor ego, it is the ultimate relief and joy for the soul. As the Twelve-Step spirituality says, 'surrender restores us to sanity'.

Full circle

When I was about six or seven years old, I put a strategic plan in place: because I reckoned God was so cruel in bringing so much sickness and suffering to our family, I decided that I would gather all the neighbours and get them to sign a petition against God! I would get the priest to announce it at Mass on Sunday and the notice would go to parishes all over the diocese and eventually all over the country. Through this signed petition, an 'ultimatum' would be issued to God – if he didn't change his ways we would all leave him. I warned him that we would leave his party, and join Fianna Fáil (for some strange reason I thought God was the leader of the Fine Gael party!).

Ironically, I have spent most of my adult life working in the area of faith development and spirituality (although I never managed to put a strategic document together with such organisational skills!). I must admit I have often identified with Saul in the scriptures, who initially persecuted the Christians and was later used as a force for working for the early Church! Unlike him, I didn't have any dazzling light, but something did certainly go full circle.

The spiritual journey often involves a stage of letting go of early practices and returning to them later in life. Sometimes, we may have to let go of 'God', in order to let God find us; we find ourselves in something similar to the space between Good Friday and Easter Sunday. This can lead to what feels like a loss of faith, but in truth it can be a deepening of faith. While we may once have discarded old practices, we often rediscover and reintegrate them in a new light, 'like a householder who brings out from his storeroom things both new and old' (Mt 13: 52).

In all of this, we do not go it alone on the spiritual journey; we are frequently sent companions. In *The Hero with a Thousand Faces*, Joseph Campbell tells us that we meet 'strangers' who are sent to help us: 'The hero is aided by supernatural power/helpers; he discovers for the first time that there is a benign power.'[58]

Strangers on the road

We were new to the village and were trying to get our bearings. I had managed to find the supermarket, the butcher and the pharmacy, but had still not found the post office or the church. We wanted to find the church to check out the Mass times for Sunday, and so we decided we would ask the next person we met for directions.

He strode along, hair in dreadlocks, studs on his nose, tattoos all over his body, wearing tattered denims. His headphones seemed to bob up and down in time to a strange rhythm. 'No point in asking the tattoo guy,' I muttered, as he approached. However, it was too late; Pat was already asking him for directions to the post office (he didn't mention the church). The stranger took off his headphones (with slight disgust, I noticed the line of studs inside his ears). He pointed to the post office, and nudged us to walk with him. As we walked along the road, he pointed out other buildings, adding, 'If you want to know where the church is, it is just up the hill, on the left. Come on, I will walk with you so you can see it.' We walked with him while he explained further, 'By the way, if you want to know Mass times, there is a ten o'clock and a twelve o'clock Mass on Sunday and nine on weekdays, and there is another church about three miles from here where there is a ten o'clock every day, except bank holidays.' We thanked him and walked away silently, wondering what we were possibly being taught here. Who was this stranger who had walked along the road with us? We were still wondering the following morning at ten o'clock Mass, when we saw, sprinting up the aisle to be a minister of the eucharist, Mister Tattoo himself!

Like us, the disciples did not recognise the stranger who 'walked with them'; only in hindsight, at the breaking of bread, did they recognise him, and their hearts burned within them (Lk 24: 32). They were surprised by fire! Likewise it was only at the breaking of bread the following morning that the significance of the encounter became a teaching moment for us. It taught us never to make assumptions about where God lives, or does not live. It taught us to remain open and sometimes willing to allow 'strangers', often those we least expect, to show us the way. Each person carries a unique revelation of the divine, and has something to show us. In *Earth Crammed with Heaven* Elizabeth Dreyer writes: 'In a profound way, our intentionality is a key ingredient determining whether we notice God everywhere or only in church or only in suffering or nowhere. It all depends on how we choose to fashion our world.'[59] Unfortunately, we often 'fashion our world' to exclude the stranger, but Parker Palmer advises us that 'God uses the stranger to shake us from our conventional points of view, to remove the scales of worldly assumptions from our eyes.'[60]

Spirituality is not some type of elevator that lifts us out of the reality of this life, but is something (or someone) that walks with us, gives us directions, breaks bread with us, and opens our eyes to recognise holy tattoos!

A God of personal encounter

This is a true story that occurred not too long ago. The farmer's sheep were stolen in the middle of the night. Some weeks later, he was sitting by the ring at the local cattle market. He saw some sheep coming out into the ring to be sold. He thought he recognised the stamp on them. Suddenly, one of the sheep tried to jump the bars to go towards him. Everyone was shocked as to why this sheep continued to try desperately to escape and make his way towards the farmer. The sheep had recognised his owner and was trying to get away from the thief who was trying to sell him. The farmer then recognised that these were his own sheep and eventually the thief was caught. This story appeared in the local papers, but what a pity the journalist wasn't familiar with the scripture piece where we are told that 'the shepherd knows his own and his own know him, they will not follow a thief or brigand' (Mt 10: 1–10). Pope Francis tells us that the true shepherd has the smell of his sheep on him! The soul knows to whom it belongs. We cannot give our life, or our love, to a set of concepts; we cannot fall in love with ideas or a set of beliefs, but only to one who knows us intimately and gives his life for us.

There is a lovely metaphor on how God kissed the soul before sending it into the world and how we are, ever since, trying to reconnect with that kiss. Like the sheep, perhaps this kiss is 'stamped' on our souls, imprinted on us, and nothing else truly satisfies until we are reunited and embraced again with that embrace. We are restless until we rest there; however, we do not have to wait until eternity – we receive many unexpected moments when we discover who we are, and so can rest in whose we are. 'The divine life is one with our life, not identical but not separate either. Thus experience of the depths of ourselves, where we are silent and free of ego, is the experience of God.'[61]

Our truest, deepest need is to be called by name, intimately known, seen and blessed. Without this blessing, we are vacillating between grandiosity and deflation, whereby we continue to ache and to bleed from the depths of ourselves. To live with a consciousness of being blessed is to see the essence of who we are, and to see everyone and everything as a blessing.

> *My fiftieth year had come and gone,*
> *I sat, a solitary man,*
> *In a crowded London shop,*
> *An open book and empty cup*
> *On a marble table-top.*
> *While on the shop and street I gazed*
> *My body of a sudden blazed;*
> *And twenty minutes more or less*
> *It seemed, so great my happiness,*
> *That I was blessed and could bless.*[62]
> – WILLIAM BUTLER YEATS

There seems to be a dehydration in the collective soul. Many are disappointed in religious practices, experiencing them as too cerebral, institutional and divorced from the heart. There is now a real call towards awakening the mystical dimension of our faith, a longing to find 'so great a happiness' that it becomes the music behind everything we do. We discover then that we are blessed and can bless.

Love is its meaning

The more we recognise that our lives are held by grace, the deeper we can trust that something will continue to hold us beyond the horizons of life as we know it. Julian of Norwich tells us that the beauty we have glimpsed on this earth will be there to meet us again when we die. She received a revelation about a wild hazelnut where she recognised that God made it, God loved it and God keeps it. 'Love was its meaning,' she said, and when asked who showed it to her, she answered, 'Love showed it to me,' Such illuminations are bittersweet: they can punctuate a moment, filling us with comfort, while also highlighting all that is passing and transient. They are not an endorsement of our own merit, nor are they a reward for any behaviour. 'A mystical experience is believed to be received as a grace. It is felt to be bestowed, not conjured at will, or generated as a result of a spiritual experience'.[63]

The ego complicates these experiences by associating them with something we have earned or achieved, or by making us feel so unworthy that we cannot even receive them. Jesus tells us, 'You know the way to the place where I am going' (Jn 14: 4). Perhaps 'we know the way' through having already experienced glimpses that are more connected with the realm of feeling and intuition than with that of logic and intellect. While we tend to yearn for their continuation and recurrence they are transient, yet they inform and guide us. The moments of passing from ordinary awareness to higher consciousness is referred to as *samadhi* in Hindu tradition. Whatever tradition we speak of, such moments of awareness are a gift.

When we look back on these moments, we discover how God has been with us all along, 'going ahead of you on the journey to find you a camping ground, by night in the fire to light your path, and in the cloud by day' (Dt 1: 33).

So, while we get no map or satnav directions, we get moments, glimpses, intimations of eternity. We seldom get the full panoramic view – scripture tells us it would be too much: 'I still have many things to say to you, but they would be too much for you to bear now' (Jn 16: 12). In the meantime, we can enjoy being surprised by those glimpses that tell us something about home and homecoming.

CHAPTER 15

Happy Ever After

The Elixir of Life

We browsed around the shops and then decided to go separately to buy the Christmas gifts for each other. 'We will take a half hour,' Pat said (who, like most men, wants to cut short the time when it comes to shopping). Off I went, thinking to myself, wouldn't it be wonderful if he bought me those classy boots in the shop window, the ones I subtly pointed out as we passed by earlier (I had even mentioned my shoe size, so he was sure to take the hint). I was in anticipatory mood as I searched for what would be an equally expensive present for him. Much less than a half an hour later, my phone beeped; a text message arrived, 'I am ready whenever you are.' I rang him. 'Where are you?' I asked. To my delight he answered, 'Remember that shop you were looking at earlier – the one with those boots you liked?' 'Yes,' I replied, holding my breath. 'Well,' he proceeded, 'If you make your way to that shop, you will find me. I am just two doors down from there – in the bookshop, at the sports section!'

I dragged my feet for the rest of the day (and continued to drag them when I got a cookbook for Christmas!). This didn't help make a happy Christmas – or a happy marriage!

Craving what we don't have and rejecting what we do have is, according to the Buddhists, one of the main sources of unhappiness. There is an inevitable disappointment when we place our happiness in the hands of what is transient and conditional. Research in modern psychology identifies a difference between the happiness that comes from an outside stimulus, and that which comes from an inner state. No doubt the perfect Christmas present can give great pleasure, but receiving any new material possession brings a very short-lived happiness. Think, for example, about the last time you bought something that you really wanted. How long did the buzz last? How long did it take before the positive emotional boost was replaced with the desire to get something else?

There is a pivotal difference between a pleasurable life (filled with possessions and pleasurable experience) and a joyful one. For a pleasurable life, certain conditions are necessary; in other words, there needs to be an outside stimulus. The problem with this is that once the stimulus disappears, the happiness tends to disappear also, and usually the stimulus creates a need for yet another stimulus, and another. (I later bought the longed-for boots myself, but now when I see them in the bottom of the wardrobe, I think to myself wouldn't it be nice to get a new pair, perhaps a different style!)

Conditional happiness

We all want great stories to end with a 'happy ever after' scenario; we hope that the prince marries the princess or that the hero amasses a great fortune. However, if we believe that happiness comes from outside of us, and is the outcome of a condition, then it is limited to that condition. Nobody is looking for a limited happiness, yet we often search for happiness in things that are limited. It seems that everything in us has been programmed to believe that happiness is synonymous with the attainment of some longed-for possession or better lifestyle. However, according to psychologist Maureen Gaffney, when we try to improve our standard of living beyond that which meets our needs, we do not actually become happier. She says that 'beyond a modest level, it is clear that investing huge time and effort in trying to increase our income and improve the material condition of our lives will not deliver greater levels of happiness'.[63] She challenges us in suggesting that if we have money to spend on luxuries, we could consider donating it to a worthwhile charity, explaining that 'this act of kindness and social solidarity will bring with it a guaranteed burst of happiness – and help make a happier society'.[64]

Perhaps equally important, if we have time to spend, we can share it with those who need a compassionate listening ear, we can sit for a while with those who are in tombs of loneliness, homelessness or addiction. Those who are stripped of their identity can be clothed anew with dignity – when we recognise that they are not a problem that needs fixing, *but human beings that need loving*. Maybe this concern for society will bring one of those 'guaranteed bursts of happiness' that we have been looking for in material accumulation.

Happy days

You know those days: you wake up, the sun is shining and you go out to greet the world with a spring in your step. You bump into somebody, greet them, get a grunt in response and you begin a tirade of mutterings – How dare she? What did I do to her? Wait until I meet her the next time! Your mood begins to descend, and for the rest of the day, you continue to feel out of sorts. Later, you bump into somebody else who cheerily gives you a compliment; your mood elevates, a temporary pseudo-relief. 'Thanks,' you say. 'You made my day.' Later that night, tiredness saps you, somebody snaps at you, and once again they unmake your day. You find yourself sliding back down again. Your mood has been like an elevator, up and down all day, depending on circumstances. You've been allowing every passing situation and event to dictate your inner equilibrium.

What is it like to be happy?

Happy people tend to be at home in their own skin; they are not overly dependent on other people or on external events for their self-esteem. This kind of happiness is deeper than that those high, frothy moods that are easily punctured. It is more like a quiet joy inside, the type of joy that you can feel on an ordinary Monday afternoon, when you feel delighted not because it's the weekend, or because you have just bought something, but because there is a joy that runs over from the inside. In other words, you feel happy just being alive and sharing that aliveness with others. An attitude like this can turn the water of your life into a lavish wine – it turns thorns into roses.

Surprised by roses

For my fiftieth birthday, I received a gift of a trip to Lisieux in France, the birthplace of St Thérèse. I had rather mixed feelings initially, since Thérèse and myself had 'fallen out' a few years earlier after I decided that she had sent too many thorns and not enough roses. (Thérèse, also known as 'The Little Flower', is often associated with roses.) Despite having greatly appreciated the profundity of what she called her 'little way', I had to eventually terminate our relationship! After some repeated stabs of her thorns, I let her have it, saying to her: 'Thérèse, we are over, it's not me, it's *you* ... I'm finished with you!'

Yet, here we are, Pat and I, sitting on the pavement in the little town of Lisieux after the train broke down on the journey back to Paris. 'Yes, Thérèse, I'm definitely finished with you now,' I shouted. 'Your *little way* really sucks!' Three hours later, tired and hungry, we got into a packed train with no empty seats (which, I presumed, was again organised by Thérèse!). It was very late when we arrived back in Paris, where we hadn't any accommodation booked for the two nights preceding our flight back to Ireland. We trudged from hotel to hotel – but as luck would have it (or, as I said sarcastically, 'as Thérèse would have it'!), the hotels were all full. 'It's fashion week,' the receptionist explained as she looked me up and down, and somehow I became acutely conscious of the grubby jumper I was wearing (which had earlier acted as a cushion while sitting on the dusty pavement at the train station). Just as we were leaving again, she said, 'I've just discovered there is a room available.' She showed us the price – to my amazement it was only a fraction of the price of any other rooms we had tried. 'It's so cheap, it's probably a dump,' I muttered as we trudged along after the porter. 'Here we are,' he said, swinging open the door (the one with the sign on it that read 'Presidential Suite'). In disbelief, I looked wide-eyed into the *four* spacious rooms, the champagne, chocolates and roses next to the coffee-maker and the huge, luxurious bathrooms. I looked at the porter and asked him if perhaps there had been a mistake. He shrugged nonchalantly and offered the key. The next two days were spent sipping champagne and eating chocolates while gazing at 'the other half' as they strolled along the Champs-Élysées. All too soon, it was time to check out, at which point we reluctantly handed back the key and paid the very modest bill. The receptionist herself seemed very baffled at how little we were being charged. She looked at the bill again before handing back the change. I decided I had better not ask too many more questions about this surprise upgrade, in case she would change her mind. Suddenly, I caught sight of a little picture at the top corner of the receipt. I put on my glasses; yes, there it was – *a rose!* 'Thank you Thérèse,' I said. 'I'm glad that your thorns can sometimes have roses.'

At the end of her life Thérèse said, 'I thank you my God for all the graces you have granted me, especially the grace of making me pass through the crucible of suffering.'[66] We too need little miracles and graces to help us pass through the difficult crucibles of growth as they augment and guide us towards the kingdom – where hopefully we will get a five-star upgrade into heaven!

Moving back the barriers
We cannot force miracles to happen, but we can sidestep the doubting voice that prevents them happening. St Augustine advised that 'miracles are not contrary to nature, but only contrary to what we know about

nature'.[67] While we cannot create a utopia, we can create actions aligned towards attracting miracles. We are not omnipotent in our ability to manifest and change the world at will, but neither are we merely passive spectators. In the gospel accounts of miracles we see that an action was often called for; the people who came to Jesus seeking miracles were themselves asked to take some leap of faith, to be co-creators of the miracle. At the changing of water into wine at the wedding feast in Cana, they were told to 'fill the jars with water' (Jn 2: 6). Small leaps of faith can move back the barriers, opening us to receive divine abundance.

Happy habits

In order to reflect on and write this chapter on happiness, I went to a quiet retreat house by the sea. When I arrived at reception, I was told there was a group of enclosed contemplative nuns there for the week. Each evening as I sat writing, I could hear peals of laughter coming from the sitting room. I eventually decided to join them for meals. I haven't laughed so much in ages, so I decided to ask them about their very obvious joy. Here is what some of them said: 'Happiness is about accepting myself as God made me, and knowing I am loved.' Another said: 'Being happy is about living in the moment, and also knowing that every place and situation has its limitation, so it only wastes energy trying to be someone else, or somewhere else.' Another joins in and says, 'Counting blessings for every day, I don't think of the things that go wrong, I just keep counting blessings.' Later, in the coffee dock, I chat with Sister Colette, a young Poor Clare sister. She is intelligent and good-humoured, and seems extroverted, yet she lives a life of silence and enclosure. She says 'happiness and joy are not the same'. She considers joy to be deeper. 'It is a gift,' she says. 'It is something we cannot manufacture, it is of the Spirit, we may not always *feel it*, but we can still transmit it.' With conviction she adds, 'A meaningful life brings joy.' She tells me that this was a huge awakening for her. She reflects on her own call and smiles, 'I have certainly been *surprised by fire.'*

I learned a lot from these inspiring women: they live a very simple life and yet they are overflowing with joy. They are here on their final few days before returning to enclosure, embarking on their 'Return Threshold'. 'Back to the real world,' one of them said last night, and while their 'real world' is a bit different from ours, we all carry the same human condition, and so the challenges are similar. While we wear different external 'habits', we espouse similar internal ones. They know what it is to do a hero's journey; by leaving behind family (when not always in accord with their choices), facing dark times, loneliness, letting go of attachments. But in all of this, they radiate joy and the gifts of the Spirit. Their 'happy ever after' is not about turning away from the problems of the world but, through love and discipline, turning fully towards it. After meeting them, I caught something of their infectious joy, and on coming away I am more motivated to 'wear their habit'!

Discipline

Changing old habits requires dedicated commitment. Discipline is a word we often resist, most likely because we associate it with willpower and steely determination, devoid of spontaneity. Discipline for the sake of itself can indeed turn life into a sterile daily grind – it can seem like a curtailment of freedom. In truth, however, it can be the most heroic type of self-mastery, whereby your energy is put at the disposal of what really matters to you. By our nature we tend to follow paths of least resistance, which can weaken our resolve to the extent that we are buffeted by every changing mood.

The plant in the hallway has a support stick to help it grow towards its potential, otherwise it falls limp and directionless. Likewise, we need healthy disciplines that act as support sticks to strengthen and direct our growth towards wholeness.

CHAPTER 16

Homeward Bound

The Return Threshold

I knew of a woman who loved going to funerals and wedding banquets. Some of the funerals she went to were for people she had never known, and she gate-crashed most of the weddings! People said that she especially loved the weddings because of the free food! She was often to be found scoffing as much of the wedding cake as she could, and putting slices into her handbag as if they were valuable treasures. Alongside the cake, she put sachets of sugar, salt and any finger food she could find into the wedding napkin and took them home (together with the wedding napkins of course!). None of this was because she was materially poor, but whatever lay behind her habit, it accompanied her to her dying days. Not long before she died, I visited her in the hospital, where, even though she was now unable to eat, she continued proudly to 'steal' the uneaten food and hospital napkins, as well as the sugar sachets and plastic knives and forks. After her death they were found, carefully hidden like buried treasures, in her dressing gown pocket!

Scripture tells us to seek the treasures that do not die when we die (Mt 6: 20). If storing up money, therefore, is your treasure, when you die people will remember you for your wealth. If becoming famous is your treasure, you will be remembered for your fame. If continuous dieting is your treasure, people will remember how thin you were! Have you ever heard people at the graveside reminiscing about the great car or the designer kitchen owned by the deceased? Unlikely. The real treasures cannot be hoarded; they are recirculated into the hearts of others. Maybe we need to think about our treasures, choosing, instead, those ones that make sure we will never die – the values and blessings we share, which will live on in the heart of everyone we meet. Henri Nouwen says the important question is: 'How can I now live so that my death will be an optimal blessing for my family, my church, and the world?'[67]

The return journey, according to Joseph Campbell, is about bringing back a gift to humankind: 'The hero shall now begin the labour of bringing the runes of wisdom, the Golden Fleece, or his sleeping princess, back into the kingdom of humanity, where the boon may rebound to the renewing of the community, the nation, the planet, or ten thousand worlds.'[69]

Perhaps you could create your own return journey; imagine yourself at your eightieth birthday party (or your ninetieth if you have passed that milestone). See yourself making a speech, recollecting the wonder of your journey, remembering especially how you turned challenges or difficulties into the 'runes of wisdom' or 'the golden fleece'.

Back where we started

The green door in front of me looked quite small now, but back then it had seemed very large. My mind returned to another time and place when that door had frosted glass. On the door, there hung a stark notice: 'No Children Allowed'. The black-and-white floor tiles were cold and sterile back then. I remembered how the smell of disinfectant used to fill the air. Counting, in my mind, the black-and-white tiles over and over again, I would try to distract myself from the green door and the sickening smell of illness. The stagnant air would occasionally be dispelled by the aroma of tea as the noisy evening trolleys passed by; on them danced clinking stainless steel teapots and tired-looking digestive biscuits. For some, there would be no biscuit tonight – perhaps only a commode or a dish for getting sick. The nurses with their white haloes and 'Sunday evening faces' would pass me by, with their starchy walks and their white 'nursey shoes', which squeaked along the cold tiles. Sometimes, they nervously followed a doctor. I used to kind of smile and genuflect to the doctors: I thought a bit of licking up to them might mean they would make my father better. But they rarely smiled back, and if they did, it was a kind of tight, withholding, 'barely tolerating' kind of smile. I would wonder why they looked so constipated, and thought it was perhaps the hospital food! I was terrified of the bulky green files that they carried under their arms. Like the door, those sickly green cardboard envelopes also seemed to hold secrets. In this enclosed, suffocating world of coughing and vomiting, one could occasionally hear sounds of another world beyond, where far away there were sounds of children playing wild and carefree games. These sounds would fade into oblivion again, only to be interrupted by a sudden beeping sound from inside the ward, then the squeak of shoes as nurses ran, with urgency, down the corridor. Then came that awful sound of someone getting violently sick. My own stomach would lurch, and I would cling desperately to my St Martin Medal, which was pinned to the inside of my cardigan. *Oh please God, or whoever is up there, don't let it be him* ... The door would open to mercilessly manifest my worst fears: it *was* him. Neither the haloed nurses nor the constipated specialists were able to perform any miracles. Sunday evenings rolled into each other, weeks, months, years; hopelessness claimed me, pervading every Sunday with a never-ending Good Friday, until his racked body could take no more and, finally, my father breathed his last.

Suddenly, I returned to the present moment, where the door resumed its proper size (only now it appeared to be much smaller). The sign 'No Children Allowed' had been taken down. In its place was a notice that read 'Guest speaker 3 p.m.; Title of talk, "Transformation: Choosing Hope".' The black-and-white tiles were not visible now as I stepped across the soft carpet. I wiped a tear from my eye, opened the door and walked in to give my presentation to the hospital chaplains and 'un-haloed' nurses. A few hours later, we were laughing and sharing the wisdom from the rubble of our lives, excavating buried treasures. My own 'return journey' and that of the participants, became shared treasure, as Campbell says, 'for the community, the nation, the planet, or ten thousand worlds'. Within our wounds lay the medicine.

Broken and blessed

We can, through engaging in our own hero's journey, turn painful, even hopeless circumstances into a beatific vision to help others. Good Friday teaches us that. When we loosen our attachment to ego and discover the divine spark within, we bring home a 'treasure trove' to humanity. All the great legends, myths and stories have this narrative running through them. Joseph Campbell tells us: 'As he crosses threshold after threshold, conquering dragon after dragon, the stature of the divinity that he summons to his highest wish increases, until it subsumes the cosmos.'[70] The 'stature of divinity' that we summon from our own brokenness becomes blessed and shared as treasure for others. This happens, not through getting rid of the painful memories, but by learning to hold them in a different way, and in a different place in our lives. We discover that, buried in the pain, there are golden seeds shimmering with divinity: 'And more important, all the life-potentialities that we never managed to bring to adult realisation, those other portions of ourself, are there; for such golden seeds do not die.'[71]

We may, of course, forever carry that 'Sunday evening sadness' tucked away somewhere in the heart, or perhaps an empty chair where a loved one once sat. However, by facing the journey, rather than turning away from it, what once seemed like stumbling blocks can become the stepping stones on the journey.

Refusing to return

At the beginning of this book, we looked at setting out on the journey, and how we are confronted with our own resistance, in what Campbell refers to as the 'refusal of the call'. Now, as we are approaching the final stage, we meet a similar dilemma, in what he calls the 'refusal to return'. This can happen in many subtle ways; we could, for example, become so intent on reaching enlightenment, or personal development, that we forget that our newfound treasures and gifts are essentially given to us for the good of humanity. Likewise, we could get so dazzled with self-reflection that we forget to return to ordinary life – a bit like the transfiguration story in the scriptures, where the disciples resisted coming back down the mountain (Mt 17: 4). The ancient Greeks used the word 'hubris' to describe one who is 'wiser than the gods'; when we get overly attached to our own wisdom we might imagine we are like little gods, wiser than others, blinded by a Pharisee complex! Beware, therefore, of those who are unwilling to reintegrate into ordinary life, especially if they begin to feel they are now 'more advanced' than the everyday Toms, Dicks and Harrys!

Those who are authentically doing the journey tend to have more presence but fewer answers, more willingness to listen, fewer certainties and more love. Compassion, humility and love are the hallmarks of one who has returned home. In the well-known story of 'The Prodigal Son', we are told that he began his return journey home when 'he came to his senses' (Lk 15: 17). Returning to our senses essentially means reconnecting with the ground of our being, our true self. We will discover that this 'ordinary place' is also the home of the Divine. As Teilhard de Chardin, author, scientist and priest, tells us, 'the deeper I descend into myself, the more I find God at the heart of my being'.[72] We will then find ourselves asking: 'How will I serve humanity?' rather than 'What does society owe me?' We will each ask ourselves how our lives can leave a magnificent trail that inspires other brave souls to make their own hero's journey? We can accept that because we have pilgrim hearts we are a bit of a metaphysical misfit in a materialistic world. Paradoxically, this is what sets us free to enjoy setting seeds, content to know that we might not always see the blossoming of the flower.

Double-edged sword

We will all, at some time, have to go through the stages of the hero's journey. It is not a once-and-for-all process; there are messy stops and starts. We often find ourselves back at square one, doing it all over again. What matters is that we keep going, that we keep following our 'yellow brick road'. Generally, the archetypal reasons for embarking on a hero's journey are to find a treasure, achieve a dream, confront a fear or change one's life. In myths and fairy tales, the reward is often symbolised with a precious pearl, some magical healing potion or a magic sword. In truth, it is often more of a double-edged sword, which cuts away the superficial life from one that is authentic, visceral and fully engaged.

After his return from the desert, we are told that Christ, 'with the power of the spirit in him, went back to Galilee; and his reputation spread throughout the countryside' (Lk 4: 14). We too have the exciting task of returning to some 'Galilee', some place where we also spread a gift 'throughout the countryside'. The homecoming journey leads us from 'me' to 'we', from the intrapersonal to the interpersonal. It is not about having finally 'arrived', because we know that we will set out on many more journeys. 'We are not converted only once in our lives', Thomas Merton tells us, 'but many times, and this endless series of large and small conversions, inner revolutions, leads us out to our transformation in Christ'.[73] T. S. Eliot also tells us that there is no final arrival:

> *We shall not cease from exploration*
> *And the end of all our exploring*
> *Will be to arrive where we started*
> *And know the place for the very first time.*[74]

Surprised by fire

In the Old Testament, the prophet Jeremiah experiences an inner fire: 'There seemed to be a fire burning in my heart, imprisoned in my bones. The effort to restrain it wearied me, I could not do it' (Jr 20: 9). Isaiah, in order to preach, had his mouth purified by red-hot coals (Is 6: 6). In the New Testament, we meet the disciples on the road to Emmaus, experiencing a fire burning in their hearts (Lk 24: 32). We are told that tongues of fire descended over each of the disciples' heads in the upper room. 'And there appeared to them tongues as of fire; these separated and came to rest on the head of each of them' (Acts 2: 3). Fire is frequently used as a symbol of the divine.

Choosing to fan the flame is the great *Amen;* it is like saying 'Thy will be done'. This is not a reluctant dragging of the feet, or a kind of 'Oh, all right so, if I must'; it is not a depressed kind of resignation, like being told to do the washing up when you really want to do something more interesting. The ignited flame isn't always dramatic or applauded by others. In fact, huge, inflammatory gestures may not be indicative of any real inner fire, but are more likely to be a compensatory strategy to gain the world's applause. When, instead, we learn to automate our lives out of the magnificent truth of who we really are, a new stillness enters our lives. Materialistic gains or ego ideals are then no longer masters, but servants, working for our greater good, and for the good of humanity. We need many more such heroes, those who give a humble but prophetic witness to the magnificence of the human spirit. In refusing the path of least resistance, we too become counter-cultural; we transmit virtues that give shape to the aspirations and longings in every human heart. Our new dignity and stillness can counteract the cultural lie that our worth resides in what we own or what we achieve.

So, while you continue to navigate this imperfect world, where there are numerous pressures, where it continues to rain too much, where the bills can seem relentless, where our bodies let us down and people let us down, you know that there is an unquenchable flame burning within. In the warmth of this inner light, you need no longer subscribe to the notion that your life is anonymous, unimportant or meaningless. You then begin to approach the ordinariness of things as parts of your life's great mosaic.

Beauty and ugliness

The nine o'clock news is blaring in the background. An earthquake in Ecuador; now the story moves to a murder; then my mind fills with concern for a friend who is finding her treatment for cancer very difficult. An evening sky, ablaze with stunning red, orange and yellow, suddenly takes my breath away. I am suffused with beauty, but then a tinge of guilt comes: How can I enjoy this beauty with all the sadness in the world? If only there wasn't so much ugliness and violence I could enjoy this sunset. No, something in me whispers, the sunset is gifting your heart, right here, right now; breathe it in. Tomorrow may rain; show up for that too.

We live in a world where there are wars, murders and earthquakes, but sunsets do not wait for some elusive perfect moment; all we can say is 'thank you', let them in, and let them go.

We must try to keep the home fires burning with hope, no matter what storms try to quench it. Vincent Van Gogh cautions that 'one must never let the fire go out in one's soul, but keep it burning'. He insists that we must guard and stoke that fire; otherwise, 'the passers-by see only a little bit of smoke coming through the chimney, and pass on their way'. [75]

Today, as I finish this book, the sun is shining, the daffodils are in full bloom, heralding the promise of spring. A couple of weeks before Easter and new life is everywhere. A car is parked in the car park of the monastery where I have been doing some writing, two small packed bags stand poignantly in the hallway; I am told they are the last few belongings of a gentle monk who is in his room waiting to be collected. I wonder what he is thinking as he hears the purr of the car engine, waiting to take him on his final journey, to the hospice for palliative care. He walks out slowly, pausing and stooping to rub the cat as if saying goodbye. The car is now moving slowly down the daffodil-lined driveway. As it slowly goes around the corner, the evening sun, for one moment, lights up the side of his face, showing eyes that seem tired, very tired, yet strangely relaxed. Maybe this is because 'home' isn't just a future state or place he is journeying towards, but a place he already knows. I relax the frown on my own face; somehow, the worries I had this morning seem less important this evening.

When it is all over, what do you want to be able to say of your life? Will you be able to say, Yes, home is a place I have embraced. Even when my eyes were tired, I didn't give up, I chose to search for the light again and again.

I went right in, stood at the edge of the naked abyss of my fear and breathed my way through it. I went all the way; I worked with what I was given. I tried to heal what limited me; I told my truth: sometimes I was loved for this, other times I was hated. I risked loving even when it meant losing. I risked losing when it meant loving. I relinquished safety and easy answers; instead I poured myself into being the best version of myself that I could be. But most of all, I can say that even though it was oft with heart pounding and knees trembling, *I stepped into the fire.*

Some day, after mastering the winds,
the waves, the tides and gravity,
we will harness for God the energies of love.
And then, for the second time,
humankind will have discovered fire.

PIERRE TEILHARD DE CHARDIN

Epilogue

'If you could have *Surprised by Fire* in as soon as *you are able,*' the publishers said. Instead of these words, I heard 'hurry up –'. 'Okay, one week,' I told myself and hardly drew a breath for a few days as I pounded, hammer and tongs, on the keyboard night and day (not even taking time to save my writing on the memory stick). A nasty flu arrived. I'll get rid of that, I said, dunking a load of lemons into a jug of hot water, whereupon I knocked the whole lot over the laptop! The laptop was destroyed – and my *unsaved* work with it! I eventually had to take to the bed with the flu and, in the silence, under the duvet, I remembered the publishers' unhurried request, 'as soon as you are able'.

Now, 450 euro poorer, I close my new laptop, and I think to myself, how is it that I write about those lessons that I, myself, most need to learn?!' In the foreword to this book, Daniel J. O' Leary writes that 'one suspects that the author is personally acquainted with some of the demons she discusses'. How right you are, Daniel! I am heartened to read that he considers my writing to be 'a passing on to others the hard-earned wisdom' of my own journey. I hope that this is so, and that, in some way, and at some time, it will light up a little corner in the heart of you, the reader. And so, as you continue to journey into the mystery, may you, with the great St Catherine of Siena, be able to say *'La mia natura è il fuoco'* *(My very nature is fire.)*

Blessings,
Martina

Flame

Wild, flaming Spirit, arise within us;
Open tired eyes,
Drag us from stale routines
Lighten our tired feet, so we can
Dance with new rhythms.

Ignite us with fire, inspire new music within us
Transfusion of Spirit, pulsating anew
May your drumbeat echo within us
Prising open the locked doors of our hearts.

Dance us out beyond old comforts
Loosen our limbs, uncoil stuck places
Send a dancing flame before us as we cross new
thresholds
And when your music quietens, cradle us tenderly
In the still centre of your Sabbath rest.

MARTINA LEHANE SHEEHAN

Notes

1. Joseph Campbell, *The Hero with a Thousand Faces*. London: Fontana Press, 1993.

2. Adapted from W. H. Murray, *The Scottish Himalayan Expedition*. London: J.M. Dent & Sons Ltd, 1951.

3. A. H. Maslow, *Religions, Values and Peak Experiences*. New York, NY: Penguin books, 1964.

4. Ignatius of Loyola, Spiritual Exercises, trans. George E. Ganss, in *Ignatius of Loyola; The Spiritual Exercises and Selected Works*, ed. George E. Ganss. Mahwah, NJ: Paulist Press, 1991, no. 333.

5. S. Lyubomirsky, *The How of Happiness: A new approach to getting the life you want*. New York, NY: Penguin Books, 2007, p. 20.

6. Martin Seligman, *Authentic Happiness: Using the New Positive Psychology to Realize Your Potential for Lasting Fulfillment*. New York, NY: Free Press Publications, 2002, p. 262.

7. www.entheos.com/quotes

8. Ronald Rolheiser, *Sacred Fire: A Vision For A Deeper Human and Christian Maturity*. New York: Image Books, a division of Random House LLC, 2014, p.200.

9. John Moriarty, *Nostos: An Autobiography*. Dublin: Lilliput Press, 2001, p. 491.

10. Jon Kabat-Zinn, *Full Catastrophic Living: How to Cope with Stress, Pain and Illness Using Mindfulness Meditation.* London: Piatkus Books Ltd, 1996, pp. 342–3.

11. Dennis Linn, Sheila Fabricant Linn, Matthew Linn, *Sleeping with Bread: Holding What Gives You Life.* Mahwah, NJ: Paulist Press, 1995, p.21.

12. Martin Seligman, *Authentic Happiness: Using the New Positive Psychology to Realize Your Potential for Lasting Fulfillment*, op. cit., p. 262.

13. Thomas Merton, *New Seeds of Contemplation.* New York, NY: New Direction books, 1972, p. 31.

14. Ibid., p. 279.

15. Brendan Kennelly, *Familiar Strangers: New & Selected Poems 1960–2004.* Hexham: Bloodaxe Books Ltd, 2004, p. 478.

16. Rainer Maria Rilke, *Rilke's Book of Hours*, trans. Anita Barrows and Joanna Macy. New York, NY: Riverhead Books, 1996, p. 88.

17. Parker Palmer, *Let Your Life Speak.* San Fransisco, CA: Jossey-Bass, 2000, p. 25.

18. Joseph Campbell, *The Hero with a Thousand Faces*, op. cit.

19. Ibid., p. 51.

20. Ibid., p. 59.

21. Rainer Maria Rilke, *Rilke's Book of Hours*, op. cit., p. 58.

22. Ibid.

23. Viktor E. Frankl, *Man's Search for Meaning*. London: Random House, 2004, p. 75.

24. Carl Jung, as quoted in John Welch, *Spiritual Pilgrims*. Mahwah, NJ: Paulist Press, 1982, p. 31.

25. Gil Boyne, *Transforming Therapy*. London: Westwood Publishing, 1989, p. 301.

26. Mark D. Sanders and Tia Sillers, 'I Hope You Dance', recorded by country singer Lee Ann Womack, 2000. Produced by Frank Liddell Mark Wright, MCA Nashville.

27. Thomas Moore, *Care of the Soul*. New York, NY: Harper Perennial, 1992, p. 216.

28. Ibid.

29. Richard Rohr, *Breathing under Water: Spirituality and the Twelve Steps*. Cincinnati, OH: Franciscan Media, 2011, p. 10.

30. Ibid., p.18.

31. Robert L. Moore, *Facing The Dragon: Confronting Personal and Spiritual Grandiosity*. Wilmette, IL: Chiron Publications, 2003, pp. 35, 36.

32. Gary McIntosh and Samuel Rima, *Overcoming the Dark Side of Leadership*. Grand Rapids, MI: Baker, 1997, p. 22.

33. Joseph Campbell, *The Hero with a Thousand Faces*, op. cit.

34. T. S. Eliot, *The Waste Land*. London: Faber & Faber, 1922, pp. 340–45.

35. Susan Anderson, *The Journey from Abandonment to Healing*. New York, NY: Berkley Books, 2000, pp. 77–78.

36. Ashley Montagu, *Touching: The Human Significance of the Skin*. Third edition, New York, NY: Harper Paperbacks, 1986, p. 126.

37. Jay R. Greenberg and Stephen A. Mitchell, *Object Relations in Psychoanalytic Theory*. Cambridge, MASS: Harvard University Press, 1983, p. 193.

38. Richard Rohr, *On the Threshold of Transformation: Daily Meditations for Men*. Chicago, IL: Loyola Press, 2010, p. 131.

39. Judith Viorst, *Necessary Losses: The loves, illusions, dependencies, and impossible expectations that all of us have to give up in order to grow*. New York, NY: Simon & Schuster, 1986, p. 29.

40. John Bradshaw, *Homecoming: Reclaiming and Championing Your Inner Child*. New York, NY: Bantam, 1990, p. 75.

41. Alice Miller, *The Drama of the Gifted Child: The Search for the True Self*, trans. Ruth Ward. New York, NY: Basic Books, 1979, 2007.

42. Pope Francis, *Laudato Si': On Care For Our Common Home*. Dublin: Veritas Publications, 2015, v. 89, p. 49.

43. Ibid.

44. Viktor E. Frankl, *Man's Search for Meaning*. London: Random House, 2004, p. 115.

45. St John of the Cross, *The Living Flame of Love, 210 Collected*

works of St John of the Cross, trans. Kieran Cavanagh & Otilio Rodriguez. Washington, DC: ICS Publications, 1991, p. 661.

46. Roberto Assagioli, 'Self Realization and Psychological Disturbances' (essay).

47. Rabindranath Tagore, *Value*. London: Unwin Brothers Ltd, 1951, p. 35; Karl Rahner, *Servants of the Lord*. New York, NY: Herder and Herder, 1968, p. 152.

48. Rainer Maria Rilke, *Rilke on Love and Other Difficulties: Translations and Consideration*. London: W.W. Norton & Company, 1994, p. 34.

49. Karl Rahner, *Servants of the Lord*, loc. cit.

50. www.entheos.com/quotes

51. St John of the Cross, 'The Spiritual Canticle', trans. Marjorie Flower. New South Wales: Varroville, 1983.

52. Daniel O'Leary, *Unmasking God: Revealing God in the Ordinary*. Dublin: Columba Press, 2012, p. 55.

53. Joseph Campbell, *The Hero with a Thousand Faces*. op. cit., p. 356.

54. Walter Sullivan, 'The Einstein Papers', *The New York Times*, 29 March 1972.

55. Carl Jung, *Modern Man in Search of a Soul*. New York, NY: Harvest/HBJ Books, 1933, p. 235.

56. Ibid.

57. Gerald G. May, *The Awakened Heart: Living Beyond Addiction*. New York, NY: HarperCollins, 1991, p. 10.

58. Joseph Campbell, *The Hero with a Thousand Faces*, op. cit., p. 97.

59. Elizabeth Dreyer, *Earth Crammed with Heaven*. Mahwah, NJ: Paulist Press, 1994, p. 23.

60. Parker Palmer, *The Company of Strangers: Christians and the Renewal of America's Public Life*. New York, NY: Crossroad, 1983, p. 59.

61. David Richo, *The Sacred Heart of The World: Restoring Mystical Devotion to Our Spiritual Life*. Mahwah, NJ: Paulist Press, 2007, p. 48.

62. W. B. Yeats, *Collected Poems*. London: Macmillan & Co. Ltd, 1963, p. 283.

63. Cited in David Richo, *The Sacred Heart of The World: Restoring Mystical Devotion to Our Spiritual Life*. op. cit., p. 88.

64. Maureen Gaffney, *Flourishing: How to achieve a deeper sense of well-being, meaning and purpose – even when facing adversity*. London: Penguin Books Ltd, 2011, p. 128.

65. Ibid., p. 125.

66. St Thérèse of Lisieux, *Story of a Soul*. trans. J. Clarke. Washington, DC: ICS Publications, 1996, p. 277.

67. St Augustine, 354–430, as quoted by Rhonda Byrne in *The Magic*. London: Simon & Schuster, 2012, p. 149.

68. Henri Nouwen, *Life of the Beloved*. New York, NY: Crossroad, 1992, pp. 92–93.

69. Joseph Campbell, *The Hero with a Thousand Faces*, op. cit., p. 193.

70. Ibid., p. 190.

71. Ibid., p. 17.

72. Pierre Teilhard de Chardin, *Writings*. Maryknoll, NY: Orbis Books, 1999, p. 50.

73. Cited by J. Pasqier, 'Experience and Conversion', *The Way*, 1977, 17:121.

74. T. S. Eliot, *Four Quartets*, from *The Complete Poems and Plays of T. S. Eliot*. London: Faber & Faber, 2004.

75. Mark Roskill, *The Letters of Vincent Van Gogh*. New York, NY: Macmillan Publishing Co., 1963, p. 110.

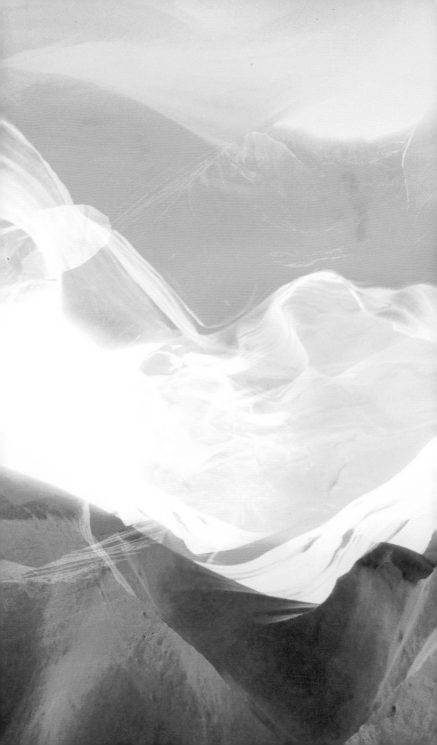